BLAIRSVILLE SENIOR HIGH SCHOOL
BLAIRSVILLE, PENNA.

DATE DUE

NOV 14			
NOV 28			
DEC 6 1988			
MY 02 '02			
GAYLORD			PRINTED IN U.S.A.

THE HUNTED CHILDREN

THE

HUNTED

CHILDREN

DONALD A. LOWRIE

NEW YORK
W · W · NORTON & COMPANY · INC ·

To the memory of martyrs, both christian and jewish, who gave their lives serving refugees in france during world war ii

CONTENTS

FOREWORD

IT IS NOT GIVEN TO MANY, IN time of war, to be engaged wholly in the preservation of values, material or spiritual, rather than in their destruction. But this was the good fortune of members of relief organizations in France during World War II. The story of that work is told here just as it happened, based on letters and notes written immediately after the events. Only, most of the names are fictitious; most of my loyal and courageous comrades of those exciting years would prefer to remain anonymous. And if my own person appears throughout the narrative it is solely because I have bowed to the publisher's wish ". . . you are going to have to resign yourself to using the first person singular . . . such a narrative has the advantage of being more immediate than any other form."

As the text shows, parts of it were written by Helen Ogden Lowrie, who also typed the whole manuscript. For this, and for her constructive counsel as the writing progressed, I can never be adequately grateful. To my sister, Josephine Lowrie, who faithfully preserved all the sometimes hasty scrawls that served as letters in wartime, goes my warmest appreciation. Monsieur Auguste Senaud provided useful summaries of the records of the World's Alliance of YMCAs in Geneva, Switzerland. For opening the files of their respective organizations in this country, I am indebted to Miss Hester Grover, American Friends Service Committee, Mr. Moses Leavitt, American Joint Distribution Committee, and Mr. Karel Sternberg, International Rescue Committee. For some of the photographs and some useful notes I have to thank Mr. Tracy Strong, Jr.; for other pictures, Martha Sharp Cogan and the AJDC. The appearance of this book is due in no small measure to William J. Haight, who by devious ways pushed me into writing it. "Too numerous to mention" are other friends, both here and abroad, who have helped in the preparation of this work. My profound gratitude goes to all of them.

D. A. L.

Knox, New York
September, 1962

THE HUNTED CHILDREN

ENGLAND

GERMANY

BELGIUM

LUXEMBOURG

English Channel

Le Havre

Cherbourg

Seine R.

Paris

Barbizon

Strasbourg

Puiseaux

Lorient

Orleans

Isdes

Tours

Sully

Loire R.

Cher R.

Châtillon
s/Indre

Atlantic Ocean

SWITZERLAND

Vichy

Annemasse

Geneva

Nontron

Lyon

x Vénissieux

ITALY

Tulle

Le Chambon

Grenoble

Argentat

Bordeaux

Dordogne

Arcachon

Garonne R.

x Septfonds

Montauban

Rhône R.

Nîmes

Vence

Biarritz

Pau

Sète

x Les Milles

Oloron

x
Vernet
de l'Arriège

x Agde

Marseilles

SPAIN

x Gurs

x Rivesaltes
Perpignan

x Argelès s/Mer

Cerbère

- Demarcation Line
x Camps
● Cities and Towns

Pétain's France
1940-1945

one

EXODUS

Life in Paris, all that spring of 1940, had moved increasingly under the sign of war, now, since the Nazi occupation of Denmark, no longer the "phony war" of the year just past. More than half the shops had closed as business wasted away, and the streets were almost empty of people—everyone not needed in the capital had gone elsewhere. After sundown the "City of light" was a faintly blue-lit ghost of itself. By day or night Paris had a strange and eerie feeling.

Then in June came Hitler's sudden plunge into Belgium, real war brought to France's doorstep, and although we all believed the Nazis would never get past the Maginot Line, tension in Paris began to mount.

After twenty years of service in various parts of Europe,

we two Americans had the feeling that it was our own home, as much as our French neighbors'. Sixteen years on the World Service staff of the YMCA in Eastern Europe and then the past six directing the United States House in the "Cité Universitaire" had given us a strong sense of belonging to this war-torn continent.

The Cité, great international student colony of the University of Paris, had emptied with the general mobilization at the outbreak of war. Some of its twenty buildings had been turned into hospitals, now beginning to receive daily transports of wounded, but, except for the Lowries still living in their spacious apartment, our House was empty as the day student life had gone out of it.

The Cité Universitaire is near the Porte d'Orléans, one of the principal southern exits from Paris. For days we had been watching the stream of cars moving away from the advancing enemy: cars loaded inside and out with families and their goods and chattels. Most of them had two or three mattresses strapped on the top. These served the double purpose of protection from machine-gun fire by enemy planes, and also something to sleep on at journey's end.

We became so used to it that this steady procession seemed almost a part of normal living, with no reason for haste in joining it. But the communiqués were daily more devastating: the enemy at Senlis and Compiègne, then at Chantilly and Château-Thierry. Allied embassies were advising their nationals to leave Paris as soon as possible. The SS *Washington* was waiting at Bordeaux to take Americans home.

Americans had no urgent reason for leaving Paris ahead of the Germans. The United States was not at war with Hitler, and he had appeared to be doing his utmost not to antagonize us. Even after the occupation of France the Nazis carefully refrained from disturbing anything American. Thus, although some Americans were caught up in the panic of flight (one prominent citizen left so hurriedly he forgot his wife), there was no panic in our departure.

America was not at war with Germany, but I was. For over a year I had been engaged in YMCA service to the French armies, especially to the Czechoslovak and Polish units. Because of my eight years in Czechoslovakia I had close contact with Czechs and Slovaks in France, and soon after the outbreak of war had found myself chairman of a committee in Paris to aid Czechoslovak citizens whose lives had been disordered by Hitler's occupation of their country. We soon had contact with a similar organization in the States, "American Friends of Czechoslovakia," and so, besides my work as representative of the YMCA, throughout the war I was director of "Czechoslovak Aid," as it was called in France. Our organization was properly registered with French authorities and assured of the sympathetic cooperation of most Frenchmen.

Now the front was moving south, and I should evidently move ahead of it, to continue service with the fighting men. No one yet dreamed that within a fortnight there would be no front.

To make the tension more merciless, Paris had sweltered for three days in heat that would do credit to a New York July and, on top of this, the whole city was bathed in a mysterious pall of greasy black smoke. It made breathing difficult. Everything one touched was black, indoors and out. Some said it was the French destroying fuel reserves; some thought it was a screen to hide the secret departure of the government to Bordeaux. When this latter rumor became a certainty, we knew we must move. "We" being the two Lowries.

After a hectic day of errands, partly to correct deficiencies we discovered in the secondhand car we had just purchased and partly to close accounts in both YMCA and Cité offices, we could consider our own preparation. The Peugeot had no baggage rack and we decided against taking mattresses. Baggage was finally reduced to four suitcases and a bundle of bed linen, leaving the rest of the space for fuel.

By special arrangement the American Legion was selling gas to Americans without ration tickets, and we filled all the cans we could buy. Then, just as we were leaving, the American Field Service men who had been living in our building, themselves packing for the same journey and for the same reasons as we, discovered two five-quart cans of gas for which they had no room, and gave them to us. Without that extra ten quarts we never would have made it to Pau. As someone remarked after the hegira, this liquid fully justified its name in French: "essence." Together with a few gas-ration tickets, it was the essential element that made possible our five-day flight.

So fortified, with a well-stocked picnic basket atop the luggage, we set out. We had decided to avoid main roads as much as possible and started out that way, but since we had been unable to buy detailed road maps for the first third of the journey, we took a wrong turning within the first half hour and landed on the main road to Fontainebleau along with thousands of others.

In spite of the terrific tension, there was no panic and surprisingly few accidents. But you may imagine the sort of driving, with three rows of vehicles of every possible sort, old or new, horse drawn or gas burning, all pushing along under the hot sun, all trying to move south as fast as possible. Occasionally someone would lose patience and break out into the one lane left for northbound traffic, in an effort to get ahead faster, but he usually came to grief and had to pull back into line. Inching along in our little Peugeot 202 in the midst of that human flood we wondered how many times we would be refugees before the war was over.

It took us six hours to reach Barbizon, usually an hour's drive from Paris, and for all that time Helen's feet were on brake and clutch, and her eyes never left the car in front. Advancing, now a few feet at a time, now a few rods, with rare stops long enough to let the engine cool, we made it at last. Despite the tragedy there was cheerfulness of a sort, and there developed a camaraderie in disaster that somehow offered moral encouragement. You would get quite friendly with people in the back of the truck beside you, piled with bedding, bird cages, water pitchers, baby cabs and children, lose sight of them again, pass and repass, and finally lose that group completely and take up with another. Here was a huge conveyor of some sort, its leather-belted arm extending twenty feet out behind, with men and women sitting on the belt clutching small bundles of clothing. Here was a whole horse-drawn village, with the mayor riding at the head of the cortege; here a family sitting at the roadside holding a figure covered with a blanket—someone too ill to move farther—what next for them?

In Barbizon most hotels were under military regulation and all the others were already jammed with refugees, but it was our good fortune to have a friend in town. Marion Greenough, in her charming place, "Les Quatre Vents," had not yet retired when we knocked at her door, and graciously took in two uninvited guests. She had not yet decided whether to join the procession moving south or to remain in her home. It was only after the war that we learned how her decision to stay had meant saving the lives of many Allied aviators, since her home became a station on the underground railroad by which flyers forced down in France could be returned via Spain and Portugal to active service in Britain.

In the morning we filled our gas tank—there was still gas at Barbizon, strange to say—swung out of town into a small road as we had planned, and found ourselves in a procession, literally touching cars both ahead and behind. We discovered that the main road was reserved for military use and all southbound traffic was congested into this one narrow artery.

A more motley procession you never saw—cars of vintages twenty years back, huge two-wheeled farm carts drawn by magnificent furry-footed Percherons from the north, with the farmer's wife and family and dog and chickens and household impedimenta all piled in together on the straw. Many of the cars had trailers, more or less improvised—one was a two-wheeled cart containing a trunk and two bird cages, and it

wobbled along on its wooden hubs, each new advance threatening to be its last. One car just in front of us had heavy silver
fox furs piled against its back window and a rusty teakettle
dangling on a string outside.

And this procession stretched out as far as one could see,
uphill and downdale, the road winding through the lovely
French countryside visible only as this long row of vehicles
one against another. The line moved literally by inches—a
sudden snort and purr of motors and your section of the file
would inch ahead, sometimes a few yards, sometimes an eighth
of a mile, then stop for a while, motors would be kept running
hopefully, then all those whose starters were in good order
would be turned off, one by one. If it was a long wait, all the
motors would stop, and then at the first snarl of a starter up
ahead, out of the older cars would leap their drivers, crank
in hand, ready to slip along another hundred feet. Across the
smiling landscape we moved in an atmosphere of exhaust
fumes. About every third car stood out as a white spot in the
dark line: these were the mattresses strapped on top.

History never saw anything like this solid caravan winding
across the landscape. Looking across the country it seemed
like a stage setting: crimson roses climbing gray stained walls;
a couple of villages on the horizon and the road twisting
across the plain toward them. The back of one antiquated
farm cart was hung with two clothes baskets full of linens
and clothes, a can of oil, and a wicker chair. As we passed we
glimpsed inside an old woman laid out on a pile of bundles,
the look of death in her eyes. She would surely not survive the
journey, probably not the day. A motorcyclist had saddlebags,
a small suitcase on behind, and a huge pack on his shoulders.
A man on a bicycle had a basket strapped to his handle bars
and on the cover, between his arms, rode a small brown dog.

And all along the road catastrophe—an antique carriage
broken down and abandoned: its occupants must have been
picked up by someone else. Motorists standing with despair
in their eyes because the gas tank was empty. This sort of

driving meant gas consumption at three times the normal rate. At every gas station, of the few still open, long queues quietly waiting for their two-gallon ration. Once after a two-hour wait we saw the station close—supply exhausted—just as we were next in line. There was a dearth of other supplies as well. After one day of this procession of misery had passed, all the shops had been picked bare. There was no disorder—what police or military authority was operative had only one slogan: "Push 'em south." Here were a young Parisian engineer and his mother, their antique motor hopelessly out of gas; they were simply shoved, baggageless, into a passing truck and told to keep moving. At this spot there happened to be a gendarme who could impose two extra passengers on a passing vehicle. Elsewhere there were dead cars of all descriptions, shoved off the road, their owners, rich and poor, hopelessly awaiting whatever might come upon them.

Then there was the bombing. Before leaving Paris we had heard rumors that the enemy was machine-gunning the slowly moving lines from the air and occasionally there was the sound of a far-off bomb explosion, but on the second day we met reality. Near what was left of a railroad station there was spread a mass of refuges, alive and dead, wrecked cars and shattered bodies, with local folk helping to care for the injured. At the town hall, the French sense of order still prevailing, clerks were issuing burial permits as fast as they could, but finally had to give up writing names and simply assigned numbers. All available men were digging communal graves. After such a machine-gun attack one man drove half a day, his dead wife beside him, before he could find a place to bury her.

All the villages along the way were alert to be helpful, to direct refugees on their way. With all the men at the front, reception duties were performed by the women and children. They would show the best road through town or indicate the hastily established shelter centers for food or sleep. All day, all night, for a week on end. And these forced pilgrims needed to be cared for; their faces were gray with weariness. Driving through this lovely farm country, many of these new exiles were reminded of their own, abandoned to the enemy. A week ago their home villages were as peaceful as these here in the midst of France. Now, all your past has crumbled, no longer has meaning, whether you are fifteen or sixty-five, and the future is a cloudy question mark. If ever you appreciated a friendly smile, or even a hot bun tossed into your cart as you passed a village bakery where flour is still available, it is now.

Never before was the French landscape more beautiful than that afternoon—there were larks in the sky, the linden trees scented all the air about them, and there was clover and a sort of heavy-perfumed laurel on the edge of the Fontainebleau Forest. About five o'clock we turned off toward a village set amid trees on a hill, to escape the crowd. A hundred other vehicles had had the same idea, but in the tiny grocery shop, almost sold out, I secured a bar of chocolate and we made tea in the village square of Romont under blossoming linden trees.

After a bit of rest we went back into line again and by nightfall had come within sight of the twisted steeple of the church at Puiseaux, about twenty miles from out starting point, ten hours earlier. We drew up in a field behind a cemetery, brewed some tea on our tiny alcohol stove, and settled ourselves in the crowded little car as best we could, for the night. Even this small side road beside the cemetery was partly barricaded, every fifty yards, by logs or huge stones so placed as to make only very slow passage possible.

The night passed quickly. Once a car tried to come up the road, saw the barricades, and turned around. It rained, and there were some flashes of lightning. Once a lost horse, evidently escaped from some convoy, came charging up the road, and went off across the fields. We awoke at first daylight, made coffee and went back to the procession. At this hour there were fewer cars on the move, though hundreds were parked at the roadside, their occupants still asleep. We could progress more rapidly than the day before. For a while we jogged along behind a light truck in the rear end of which, behind a mattress piled on some chicken crates and a stack of cooking utensils, a rosy-cheeked boy half sat, half lay, with a black and white setter on his lap, both fast asleep.

In the middle of the forest above Sully a big truck had stopped, and a family was unloading a demountable house, evidently planning to settle there. As we neared the Loire, traffic was almost as congested as the day before, but by eight o'clock we were in sight of the bridge and crossed it a half hour later. Afterward we learned that the French blew up that bridge an hour after we crossed it. Immediately the road seemed to clear and we could move along more easily. In the not very interesting-looking village of Isdes we bought two pounds of fresh bread, the first we had been able to get since leaving Paris. We had coffee in a small café with a barbershop attached, and the proprietor let me shave myself while he helped his wife with the dishes.

At Châtillon-sur-Indre we stopped for tea in the one hotel mentioned in the guidebook. Like all the other towns, it was jammed with refugees, not of this procession but of those displaced earlier. There were loads of Alsatians, already pretty well acclimated after living here since September, and Belgians who had arrived three weeks earlier. Here we discovered a garage that still had gas to sell and bought our two-gallon gas ration. Later we joyfully waited three hours in line to acquire another whole gallon. We went around to another hotel and asked the proprietor's advice. "You won't find any rooms in this town," he told us, "but just drive out into the country and ask at almost any farmhouse."

So an hour later we turned off on a side road and stopped under a vast mountain of a linden tree, heavy with bloom and droning with bees, foliage so thick the rain could not get through. At the farmhouse nearby we asked the farmer's wife's permission to spend the night in the car under that tree. "But you'll be more comfortable in the barn," she insisted. "I'll put a feather bed on the floor, and you will be out of the

rain at least." Soon she had helped arrange a feather mattress
on the earthen floor, with fresh straw for carpet around it,
and a great stack of new-mown hay perfuming the whole
place. She brought a blanket and bolster, we put down our
steamer rugs, and the dormitory was ready. We had bread
and cheese for supper just inside the open door, on a table
improvised from two upturned baskets, and watched the rain
patter down into the morass that was the farmyard.

It was 8:30 when we turned in and slept like the dead until
next morning, despite farmyard noise and odors. A scanty
toilet made possible by a trip to the well with a bucket bor-
rowed from the farmhouse, and we were ready for the breakfast that the farmer's wife had offered to serve: huge bowls of
a brown liquid called coffee and slices of homemade bread,
consumed beside an open fire where the noonday soup was
cooking on a crane. As everywhere, these people were greatly
depressed by the news that the French army was still retreat-
ing. Their one son was last heard of in the front near Reims
and for weeks there had been no news.

Every town along the way was crowded with refugees,
mostly of a month back, but already some from this new
hegira. In one village we talked with a pleasant Dutch lady
who had been on the way from Holland a month. "I had permission to stay here two weeks," she told us, "but now I must
move on, and I wonder where I can go." It was odd to see a
lady in a fine silk print dress, coming along from the village
wash trough with a lot of clothes she had been laundering.
Everywhere other refugees were asking where we were bound
for, as though they hoped to learn of some unoccupied corner
in France.

At the neat town of Nontron the Peugeot began to have
coughing spells. A garageman agreed to send to Périgueux for
the necessary spare part, and told us we would be able to go
on the next afternoon.

A town with such a negative-sounding name seemed to
promise little help for weary travelers, and a round of the few

hotels made this certain. Here I bethought me of my official connection with the University of Paris and went to call on the director of a state apprentice school on the edge of town. We could not have been more generously received if we had been rich cousins here on invitation. All the boarding pupils had left the previous day and, moreover, there was a guest room with a bath and even hot water. Monsieur and Madame Picot took us into the family, invited us to dine with them, and we spent a delightful evening.

The whole village was burdened with the calamity. Stray groups of lost soldiers stood at street corners. Every few minutes a troop transport went by, pushing south. A column of trucks, first an air unit and then some regimental office— screeching horns to clear the passage. As they roared past his shop opposite the school, the local baker would toss a half dozen buns into the hands of the four men crowded into the front seat of each.

The garageman was as good as his word, and after lunch with the Picots we got off to an afternoon of flat tires. Our jack was out of order, and this meant walking to the nearest town and imploring someone to bicycle out, breasting the flood of traffic, and change the tire. Twice that afternoon it happened, the second time late in the evening, and it was Saturday: no workmen available. One garageman gave us to understand that as the proprietor of the shop he could not bother with changing tires. But he had a folding bed in one corner of the garage, his kindly wife put down an old mattress on the concrete floor, and the next morning the proprietor himself spent hours to accomplish a miracle of repair work, against obstacles like a breakdown of the town's ancient power plant and a spare inner tube that turned out to be the wrong size. When we asked for the bill, the man said, "Three patches, that's twelve francs" (24 cents).

One more village stop where, although it was a Sunday, a cheerful little man sold us a tire and a jack, and the big road to Pau was fairly free of traffic. By a bit of foresight unusual

in our family I had visited Pau some weeks earlier and rented
an apartment where we could store office files and some of
our own trunks, or even ourselves, should circumstances re-
quire it. Earlier in the war all this baggage had been kept in a
small country villa north of Paris, which we thought of using
as a weekend retreat or housing if Paris should be bombed.
Then, about a week before the Germans took the city, we
discovered that our villa lay directly in the path of their advance, so we hastily removed the file cases and trunks and
shipped them by railroad express to Pau. When we reached
the city gates we learned that no one without a place to live
could be admitted to the city; all available shelters were full.
By proving that we had a vacant apartment at our disposal,
we easily passed the barrier and the sixth night of our hegira
could spread our blankets to sleep on the floor of our own
domicile.

Looking back on it, what stood out in memory were the
lovely French landscapes and the catch in one's throat every
time one looked on that beauty and recalled the unheard-of
disaster at that moment stalking across the country; the unfailing courtesy of other travelers, despite their drawn and
worried faces; the amazing hospitality and kindness to strangers: a tragic journey ministered to by a neighborliness
unforgettable.

two

JUST INSIDE
THE LINE

THE EXODUS CAME TO AN ABRUPT
end, as enemy tanks rolled down the coast past Bordeaux,
through Biarritz, to the Spanish frontier. The armistice fixed
the famous "demarcation line" that just bypassed Pau, leaving
it in the unoccupied zone, and led across France to the Swiss
border, with Vichy, the new capital, within reach of German
artillery should this be needed. There was considerable moving about in "free" France, but everywhere all possible shelter
was so crowded that search for something better was useless
and most refugees sat down wherever they were at the end of
the war, unwanted guests in the community. By this time
two and a half million French had been evacuated or had fled
from northern France and over a million Dutch and Belgians
had piled in with them. The number of aliens now in France

was one tenth of the total population.

Pau, France's most British city, where hunters still rode to hounds, somehow managed to preserve its traditional calm amidst crowding disaster. The city's whole setting was peaceful, the inspiring view over the sunny chain of the snow-topped Pyrenees, the amazing variety and luxuriance of its vegetation, palms and bamboo growing alongside oak and maple. Walking along the Boulevard des Pyrénées, I noted the humming of bees in the full-flowered, fragrant lindens and thought that here was one group of workers undisturbed by the general calamity.

In Pau we were rather privileged refugees. We had our own roof over our heads; five other friends from Paris made us only seven people in four small rooms, and we quickly adjusted to the new order of living. It was strange not to have to darken all windows at night. The first piece of furniture we bought was a radio. All French broadcasting was forbidden by the cease-fire terms, and now, as throughout the war, the BBC was our one dependable source of information. We could, on occasion, listen in on broadcasts of "neutral" news from America. Blankets and a few chairs and a kitchen table were bought somewhat later. These essential housekeeping occupations helped fill the first few days, but they were days of stunned waiting in an atmosphere of tension almost indescribable. For France the war had ended, but no one knew what would come next. What would an armistice, if there was to to be one, bring us? The leaden atmosphere paralyzed all initiative: it was days before we could manage to write even intimate friends.

The stoicism with which the French people were bearing this most tragic moment in their history was amazing. No one could understand how this could happen. They had known their army was Europe's finest, and the Maginot Line impregnable, and now—? Most French people did not want to make any kind of terms with the Nazis, until further resistance had proved such an act inevitable. But in the meantime every-

one was at his post, doing his daily tasks, and helping others
as much as he could.

Then came the dreadful 25th of June, the Day of National
Mourning decreed for the publication of the armistice terms
with Germany. Rumors of these terms had been abroad for
days, and we had heard them by way of the London radio
the night before, but even after publication most French
people were too stunned to comprehend the full import.
There was a stillness over all the town like a Sunday, as I
made my way through the quiet crowds toward the post
office. No one who did not live through it can imagine what
it was like: disaster and defeat quite unthinkable even a fortnight before, had wounded spirits so that those of us who
shared their sorrow overlying our own were ourselves almost
prostrate. Men would try to tell you what it meant to any
Frenchman, and would weep quietly as they talked. Women
with drawn faces went about the streets like shadows. Most
people felt it was wrong to sign a formal armistice: they were
sure the whole of France would be occupied, or in any case
dominated, by Hitler, so there was no need to agree to it in
advance, and on such shameful terms. In the main hall of the
post office, where the armistice terms were posted, I counted
nearly a hundred people, all in their Sunday black, but there
was a hush over the place as in the sickroom of a patient mor-
tally stricken.

All the suffering, mass or individual, was multiplied by the
disorder in all branches of government and supply. Rail and
mail services were only partially in function, although some
of them carried on in the midst of the general disorder, by
virtue of inertia. Two days before we left Paris we had shipped
our trunks by railway express to Pau. Then came the debacle,
with the railway lines from Paris in enemy hands, and we
mentally added the loss of that baggage to all the rest of the
property we had left behind. A chance remark by another
refugee led us to call at the express office ten days after we
reached Pau, and soon the express truck delivered our bag-

gage intact, as though it had been transported in the most peaceful of summer vacations.

Some sections of the government moved four or five times before landing in Vichy, each time more precipitately than the last, and records and personnel were lost at each move. Added to this was the terrible uncertainty that haunted every family. In the immense confusion of evacuation and retreat, literally millions of families had become dispersed: about two million were prisoners of war or missing. During the exodus more households became separated, so that there was scarcely a family in France without its share of intense anxiety for some lost member.

The single-sheet newspapers carried cramped little ads: "Madame Jean Goullot informs her husband that she is with cousin Marie. Children well." "Three-year-old boy, giving the name Jean Tavares, was found alone in a wheat field at Isdes, morning of June 18. His parents please communicate." "Madame Pierre La Grange implores anyone knowing whereabouts of her husband to write box 127. Left military hospital, Fontainebleau during exodus. Last seen near Sully wearing yellow leather coat." Repeat this a million times, and that is what France was like in the weeks following the armistice.

For many refugees there was no hope of finding lost kinfolk. One day shortly after we reached Pau, Helen and I met the Warschauers, old friends from Belgium. They, too, had lived through the exodus, having made the journey in a small car all the way from Brussels, with more terrible experiences than ours. One day, not far from the bombed-out station we had passed, they came upon a vast splash of wrecked vehicles on and off the road, riddled by machine-gun fire from a passing enemy plane. Near one car stood a small girl, eyes wide with fright, beside the bodies of her parents. Another stoppage of the procession brought the Warschauers to a halt beside her. "What should we do?" the man asked his wife. "Maybe someone else will pick her up," she said with a gesture toward the other lines of cars, now beginning to move again—"with our crowded car—" "But we can't leave her alone—" and their small car now carried another passenger. "We'll leave her at the next reception center," they told each other. Instead, "Masha" rode with them three days.

And when they arrived in Pau Masha was their first concern. They told us the rest of the story: "We took her in, but in three days we hadn't been able to find out much about her. Conversation en route was difficult, for the little girl spoke only a language that we recognized as Russian. She told us her name was Masha, but beyond that could give no more family data than could most other three-year-olds. She had somehow accepted this travel with strangers, and although she sometimes wakened us at night crying 'Mama,' she rode quietly, big eyes taking in all the details of the road, but saying almost nothing we could understand."

As the Warschauers registered, upon their arrival in Pau, they explained to the police secretary: "This is a little girl we picked up along the road. We don't know anything about her except that she seems to be Russian and her name is Masha. In our circumstances we, of course, cannot continue responsibility for the little thing—there must be some orphans' home that would take her in."

"There is, and a good one, too, from what I hear," the officer said. "My wife is on a committee that helps a Russian children's colony out here in the country about twenty miles, and she's always telling everybody what a remarkable operation it is. Why not keep the child until tomorrow—with this milling crowd I can't do anything about her now—and I'll ask my wife to talk with you. Come around about ten tomorrow morning."

The next afternoon the Warschauers met a bright-faced matron who spoke to Masha in Russian. The little girl ran into her arms, and looked around only long enough to say good-by to her rescuers. She never saw them again. So Masha joined the other Russian children in the Château de Claracq.

As one of its founders I had since 1922 been interested in

the Russian Student Christian Movement with their extensive
youth program. Their success in maintaining Russian Christian
culture among Russian émigrés in the decades when such
activity was impossible in the Soviet Union had been remarkable. In the ominous summer of 1939 they had conducted
their usual summer camps for younger and older children, one
in the mountains near Grenoble and the other on the Riviera.
Then the war started, and all the children of school age were
evacuated from Paris. The camp season finished, but the authorities could not permit these Russian children to return to
Paris. The camp leaders were at a dead end: they could
neither stay where they were—both camps were in a milita-
rized zone—nor return home. The camp budget had been
calculated at an absolute minimum, including special excursion
rates for the return trip. Now there was no cash on hand to
feed the children or to pay their transportation to wherever
they might be allowed to go.

Thanks to generous aid from the French government, and
to some new-found friends—the Russian-American Save the
Children Fund and others—the two camps could be moved
first to temporary quarters and then across France to lodge
near Pau. For the youngsters of high school age a villa on the
edge of town was rented, and the others, sixty of them, were
put down in a rickety old château named Claracq. When I
first saw it, in December (1939), I thought the only thing to
do would be to move those children out of it as soon as possible.
The place had not been lived in for years: wallpaper was
dripping from the walls; the water system was out of order.
Doors and windows did not fit their frames and there was no
furniture except the makeshift beds the group had brought
from camp, and the scantiest excuse for bedding. It was
already cold at night and most children had only their summer
clothes, and those worn thin. The whole place smelled of
decay and dreariness.

A few months later, when I arrived in Pau via the exodus,
I saw that the young Russian leaders had accomplished a

miracle. Over a hundred children lived at Claracq; besides the sixty who had been in camp, many others had arrived from Paris during the winter. The dingy rooms had been done over, there were better beds, and even some other furniture. All the floors had been refinished and there was a charming house chapel with gold-framed icons. A priest had come with the children from the Grenoble camp. There was a regular French school with a teacher provided by the Ministry of Education. In wartime thousands of children had been moved out of cities and big towns and in order not to disrupt their education the government supplied teachers wherever a group settled.

You might think that handling a hundred children after what these had just lived through would create unconquerable difficulties, but it did not work out that way. There was good order and discipline, especially noteworthy because, as the leaders knew, some of the Paris children had lived under conditions of almost unbelievable neglect. A striking improvement in their manners and conduct was soon evident. I once asked the directress what she thought was Claracq's greatest success, and she said "the improvement in the children themselves."

The older boys and girls who lived in Pau showed the same progress. Our RSCM Committee rented a second villa, and the boys lived there, taking their meals with the girls in the first house. They also had a chapel, in what once was the garage of the villa. The boys made some neat furniture and decorated their rooms, although the poverty was such that if a pair of shoes needed mending the owner had to stay away from school until repairs were done. School reports were good, some of the girls, especially, stood at the heads of their classes. I had been able to provide a small library of Russian classics.

You should have heard these young people sing! I have heard it said that when two Russians are gathered together, there is a discussion; when there are three, there is a schism; but when there are four, there is a choir, and harmony again. We had a choir. It happened that the matron in charge of the teenagers in town was a former opera soloist. She built that group into a chorus good enough for the concert stage. On one of my visits they gave us an impromptu recital, with Russian songs ranging all the way from 15th-century church music to songs of the homeless boys in Soviet Russia. A benefit concert given for the Red Cross was a great success.

Facing the penury of foodstuffs already keenly felt, the task of supplying a colony of children was not easy. The French Red Cross helped as much as it could. The Americans on our Claracq committee got some supplies from the American Red Cross and the boys spaded up the garden to provide all the vegetables needed throughout the summer. Even then, our feeding problem caused us much concern. It was difficult to feed children on the government allowance of twelve cents per day.

Through the troubled prewar years France had remained true to her motto of liberty, equality and fraternity. Never had her door been shut to those who sought asylum. Almost before World War I ended, the Russians had begun to come, fleeing the terror that raged in their homeland. Italian fugitives came next, men and women of too-liberal ideals to feel at home with fascism. Then came refugees, Jews and Gentiles both, forced out of Germany by the fantastic cruelties of Hitlerism. Then they came from Spain and Ethiopia. Then such Czechs as were able to escape Nazi "protection," and the Poles driven from home by the combined action of two of the greatest gangsters in history. And now this new flood of misery from Holland and Belgium. Even after the cease-fire, as it became evident that the whole Atlantic coast would be occupied by the enemy, new refugees from there came crowding in.

Americans engaged in this relief work felt that somehow we were carrying a tiny part of what should be our country's share of the refugee burden. For by this time, refugees ourselves, we had become relief workers as well. In the days immediately following the armistice, American Red Cross representatives passing through Pau had appointed me their agent for a study of the relief needs of our province, and shortly thereafter transferred funds for our use as the situation would seem to indicate. Thus for the rest of those tumultuous weeks in Pau I wore three hats: YMCA, Czech Aid and ARC.

Every town, every village, was full of refugees, French or foreign. The collapse of France caught a thousand young men and boys who had been grouped in Toulouse for transport to farms and factories, with no authority now responsible for their care. A Quaker report of those days said: "They need everything. We cannot hope to help half of them. . . . Montpellier is so crammed that our people have had to go eighteen miles out of town to find a bed. Toulouse is stripped of all necessities, with nothing coming in by rail save more refugees."

Pau, normally a city of only forty thousand, handled its tens of thousands of refugees with admirable organization. A series of special dormitories was fitted up in theaters, dance halls and schools. Fortunately this was summer and schoolrooms were vacant. There were even blankets on the cots. And every bed occupied. Women and children, men and boys, most of them with all their possessions in a small bundle beside them, slept like the dead, after days and days of tormented flight. Women's organizations in the city set up cheap feeding kitchens. As soon as newcomers were registered, the authorities moved most of them in busloads to outlying villages, to make room for the next wave of fugitives. Abandoned farmhouses or vacant schools had been hastily equipped to house the newcomers, and each community took over the job of feeding them, no small task for towns with no hint of an organized charity budget. To several of these excellent volunteer organizations we were able to make contributions from American Red Cross funds. And everywhere we found the same sort of human kindness as we had encountered on our comparatively easy journey from Paris.

One day we met a group of Czechs arrived here on bicycles after eight days on the road. They were machine-gunned a dozen times. A woman from Paris was sixteen days on the

way, walking over two hundred miles of the distance pushing
a bicycle, since she had a seventeen-year-old girl in charge,
and the girl had no wheel. In the confusion of a bombing the
two were separated, and this woman hadn't seen the girl since.

Some refugees had happier stories. One day in a café in
Pau I made the acquaintance of a French officer, now demobilized and waiting for a chance to go abroad. His story had
a cheerful ending.

"I have a capable wife. Before I married I said to myself:
'I may be able to have children, but I cannot be bothered with
raising them. Therefore I must pick a clever wife who is a
good manager. And I think you will agree that I found one.
I have just received her letter smuggled across the line, my
first message in two months. A while back I bought a small
farm in Normandy, and not long before the German attack
on Belgium I sent my wife and three small boys to live there.
Having seen all too much of refugees all over Europe, I told
my wife to stay on the farm no matter what happened. Well,
she did until the evening when shells began to fall all around
the town, and most of the population had already fled. Then
she decided it was time to move. In a shed she discovered an
old car of the vintage of 1930, all its tires flat and the lights out
of order. She had never driven a car in her life, but she found
an old man who repaired the tires, gave her a half hour's lesson
in driving, and she set out.

"You know what the roads were like: one solid mass of
vehicles, mostly army trucks, careening along at eighty kilometers an hour. She barged out into this procession, doing a
hesitant fifteen. Nevertheless, she kept the car going until
within sight of Tours, when it finally broke down and she
could do nothing with it. She sent word to friends in the city
who were themselves on the point of leaving. They came out
with their car and took her and the three boys with them,
stopping at Arcachon where enemy columns flooded past
them. Instead of fleeing farther after the armistice, as many
of her friends did, my wife stayed in Arcachon, and within

four days had managed to acquire permission from the German authorities to return to her Normandy farm. She found it unharmed and got back to it before pillaging had begun, apparently none the worse for her experience."

Adding to the general confusion in Pau were the thousands of lost soldiers: men who were already demobilized but could not return to their homes in the north or men who had lost contact with their units in the tumultuous retreat before the enemy. Dusty and rumpled, they sat at all the street corners or moved aimlessly about the city. The garrison barracks gave them food and lodging, but no pocket money, and the need for some sort of club or "foyer du soldat," as the French call it, was evident. Out on the Casino terrace, facing a view of the snowy Pyrenees, was a large hall with kitchen and other accessory equipment. When we called on General A., commanding the Pau district, to ask permission to use the Casino for a serviceman's club, he was so moved that his eyes filled with tears. ". . . that anyone, and especially Americans, would come with an offer of help in a time like this . . ." he said, and we were assured of the fullest support from the authorities.

Fortunately, almost all the furniture and equipment needed for this enterprise was already in place; otherwise it would have been quite unobtainable in this town where every scrap of secondhand furniture had been bought up by or for the refugees. There were roomy lounges with crystal chandeliers, a vast café where we could serve such drinks as were available and sketchy-looking sandwiches or packets of dry sweet biscuits. There was even a movie theater. For staff we appealed to women's organizations in the city's churches and to the local chapter of the French Red Cross. The women gladly responded, and soon the place was abuzz with soldier business from morning to midnight. The only items we did not provide for these throngs of disoriented soldiers were beds. The Casino soon became the most important military rendezvous in town. One of its striking features was its row of bulletin boards, where any soldier could leave a message. "All men of the

Chasseurs Alpins should report to that office in Oloron."
"Anyone knowing the whereabouts of the 2nd Company, 1st
Regiment of the Zouaves leave word at the desk." In the midst
of an atmosphere almost like shell shock on a national scale
the club somehow gave a welcome sense of order and stability.

General A. could be stern as well as tender. It happened
that the same day we called on him the Germans made their
first appearance in Pau. This was a "normal" official visit,
since Pau was the capital of a province whose coastal areas
were under occupation. The Germans arrived in an armored
car escorted by motorcycle machine gunners. The general
refused to see them. "Come in your official cars, like gentlemen," he had them told, "and you will be received."

three

PASSPORTS AND MILK

ABOUT THE TIME WE REACHED
Pau word went out that all American passports must be
exchanged for new ones at an American consular office. Our
nearest consul was in Bordeaux, and on a Sunday morning we
set out, although the Germans were reported as nearing the
city. We had spent most of Saturday securing necessary
travel permits and gasoline tickets. Orders concerning the
sale of gas were changed three times in the course of the day,
which did not make preparations any easier. No nonmilitary
vehicles were permitted to move on Sundays (part of the gas-
rationing scheme), so we needed a special military permit.
Ours was almost the only civilian vehicle on the road. There
were columns of dusty army trucks still moving southward
with troops and equipment being saved from the enemy.

Detachments of soldiers wandered along the streets of every town: many of them had not seen their officers for days. Everywhere was a sense of disorientation and lack of purpose. No one knew what he should do next.

When we arrived in Bordeaux we could hear the enemy guns, just a few miles to the north, but the American consulate was still functioning. For two of the three in our party passports were issued at once, but I had no photo with a light background, as regulations required, and the vice-consul refused to consider any of the others I presented. On Sunday no photographers could be found to take a new picture. It was manifestly impossible for me to come a second time to Bordeaux—the Germans would be there within thirty-six hours—but this made no difference to our brave vice-consul. He was adamant: no proper photo, no passport—one of the finest examples of consummate bureaucracy in my experience.

This explains why, a few days later, armed with a regulation passport photo made in Pau, I set out for Marseilles, now the nearest consulate, hundreds of miles away across southern France. Of course I had to have a travel permit. The usual procedure to obtain such a document necessitated days of waiting in stuffy anterooms, inquisitorial questioning by some not always polite functionary, near-frantic efforts to find the required personal documents or satisfactory substitutes. How could you prove, for instance, that you had never been in jail in your home town, now behind the demarcation line? Or what sort of justification could you proffer for a trip to Marseilles, when railroad traffic was already overburdened and the lack of axle grease was daily reducing the number of trains that could run? After that it would be weeks, often months, while applications went to Vichy, perhaps getting lost en route and thus requiring a new start and fresh copies of all the documents.

This was routine for ordinary mortals: for an American representing a well-known organization the procedure was simplified. It took me only three days, what with some secretary's being ill and another typist overworked, and eventually I was fully equipped with documents bearing my photograph, my signature attested by a police seal, and a rubber stamp from the Prefecture and could set out on my first railroad journey in post-armistice France.

I discovered that each section of the railroad was a kingdom unto itself: I could learn what time my train was due in Toulouse where I had to change, but I would have to wait until I reached there to discover what connections I could make for Marseilles. A demobilized soldier in the Pau station assured me that I should count on about eight hours between trains every time I had to transfer. The soldier was one of a group of thirty, soiled winter uniforms hung about with a dozen nondescript bundles, who had just spent twelve hours standing at a small junction. This was five o'clock in the evening, and their next train would leave at two in the morning. They swore a bit, but at once began looking about the smelly station, as scores of other people, civilian or military, were doing, trying to find a place to dump their bundles in a heap and sleep on them until traintime.

Since our train was made up at Pau, it started on time and had the additional advantage that if one arrived at the station early enough one was assured of a seat. Before we reached Toulouse, twelve hours later, not only was every seat occupied, including the toilets, but the corridor was so full of standees that it cost a small battle to pass through. The general atmosphere of camaraderie in distress reminded one of the exodus.

In Marseilles I found that the American consulate had been moved out on the edge of the city, partly to obtain more office space, partly, one heard, to lessen the size of the patient mob that clustered around the entrance, Austrians and Spaniards and Czechs and others, all ages and all conditions, hoping against hope that some special providence had intervened since their last call here and that a visa to America could now be given them. My American passport, waved in the air, made way for me through the crowd, and soon I was talking with a consul vastly more sympathetic than that stuffy bureaucrat in Bordeaux. He issued my new passport at once, but remarked that it would probably be used only for return to the States. "New United States regulations prohibit the transfer of any funds to France," he told me, "so that even if you decided to remain here you would have nothing to work with. The United States government wishes all nonmilitary American citizens to return home."

This was it, and it was official, so I composed a cablegram embodying the consul's remarks and dispatched it through official channels—consulate to State Department to the New York YMCA headquarters: we were returning home. Fortunately, an official cable was assured a leisurely journey, for about the time it reached New York, another we had sent from Pau by open wire stated: "Ignore first cable. We are remaining France, letter follows."

This right-about-face was due to the Waitstill Sharps, representing the Unitarian Service Committee on a mission of service to France. They had to wait three weeks in Lisbon for the requisite travel permits (neutral Portugal was the most direct approach to unoccupied France for travelers from the States). This delay gave the Sharps time to study the relief situation in France. What with disrupted transport and the separation of the dairy regions of the north from the wine-growing south, milk for babies was clearly one of the most urgent requirements. The Sharps promptly bought a carload of canned milk in Lisbon and, aided by the American Red Cross and Portuguese and Spanish Red Cross Societies, got it transported to France in what for those days was record time.

Waitstill and Martha came on ahead of the shipment and I met them on their arrival in Marseilles. They wondered where their carload of milk could be distributed to do the most good. Because I had seen how the refugees, like swarms of locusts, had eaten up every sort of food available in that corner of France, I suggested Pau. It was American Red Cross policy to make no distribution in an occupied or partly occupied province, so no help for the Pau situation could be expected from that source. In Pau our good contacts with the authorities would facilitate distribution, and so the freight car was routed across southern France from Port Bou to Pau, and Martha Sharp went at once to make detailed plans on the spot.

Martha met Helen in Pau, and a friendship began that has never failed since. Together they planned and conducted a relief action that the French Red Cross considered a model of order and effectiveness. If you were writing a book about it, the title might be *Mayors and Midwives*, and it would describe the survey of needs, the careful allocation of supplies, and the actual delivery of that precious milk.

The first thing we had to do was to wangle some gasoline for the small Peugeot so that Martha and Helen could visit the villages. It took eight separate calls on various city or department offices, but after presenting an itinerary with the distances indicated they got an allotment of forty liters (about ten gallons) and came out even after visiting more than twenty villages and doing 240 miles. Armed with the names of the midwives and visiting nurses in these villages provided by the doctor at the head of the Hygiene Service and the chief of the Public Health and Social Welfare Service, Martha and Helen started out to see the world as it concerned the babies of the Basses-Pyrénées.

They went into small homes, squalid and sordid on the outside, to find old family furniture, polished with age, shining copper kettles, and cleanliness and order; into larger places with lambrequins and plush pillows, artificial flowers, and silk squares dripping from the lampshades. Some women had dressed up to meet them, others were a bit frowsy and out at the elbows. One grand lady (not a midwife, but the president of her section of the French Red Cross) lived in a château before whose gates they sat while the lodgekeeper carried their card to the house to find out if they should be admitted. They were (eighteen tons of milk is an open-sesame), and found a gracious hostess surrounded by beautiful family antiques. To be sure, she had kept them waiting while she got into suitable clothes, but she evidently forgot to change her stockings, which were thick cotton and hardly appropriate with her print silk dress! One midwife received them with all her family: husband and children. Now and then a husband seemed to have as much to say about his wife's profession as she herself, and proudly read out of her book the number of births during the year, the proportion of babies who needed supplementary feeding and those ill because there was no good milk in the district.

Martha and Helen had sent out a questionnaire and an announcement of their visit and one village provided an entertaining welcome. The two women had stopped at the pharmacy on the square to inquire where the midwife lived, and while they were there the town crier appeared, beating his drum, and announced that mothers with babies who needed canned milk should assemble at a certain place that afternoon at 3:15. This was swift action! It looked as though the midwife must be expecting the cases of canned milk to arrive in that small car. But it turned out that this was only her method of finding out the answers to some of the questions, and later the ladies in Pau received the information, collected as a result of the town crier's announcement. A typical report on the questionnaire came from the visiting nurse of the village of Nay: of the children in that village, under two years of age, 43 were native and 61 refugees.

The midwives proved to be well trained and devoted to their work. They talked with pride of their little charges, and of those who could not do well on the present poor quality of milk. In one town which was particularly crowded with refugees, the visiting nurse pleaded for solid alcohol so that the mothers living in one room could heat milk for their babies. Another midwife, who had a "beat" of twenty communities to take care of, hoped she could have plenty of "farine lacté," "Pablum" in English, because she had so many babies with eczema. One beautiful child was covered with a rash which seemed to be mosquito bites, or worse, but which the nurse said was caused by lack of butter and fat in the child's diet. Another visiting nurse turned out to be the schoolmistress who, when she came to that village seventeen years before, had found such an appalling lack of knowledge about infant care that she had studied it herself and had begun holding clinics to help the mothers take care of their babies. She said it had been hard going at first, but finally the women had come to feel a pride in their well-cared-for children and now there was real competition among them. The schoolmistress had organized a workshop where the women could meet and sew for their families, and the older girls in the school also learned something of child care. When the refugees flooded the town, this woman immediately formed a playground for the young children and later a workshop for those unfortunate families who had left everything behind them. She will always stand out in memory as one of the finest women encountered on the trip. Another woman who owned a large house had turned it into a hospital and with volunteer help from refugee nurses was running a thirty-bed hospital with a flourishing maternity ward.

Another institution was the Pouponnière, Doll's House, operated by the Health Department, where abandoned babies were nursed through their first infancy and then put with families when well started on their way. The inspector of public health was the legal guardian of all these little waifs and a prouder man was never seen when he talked about his Pouponnière. And it was a charming place, set high on a hill with the range of the Pyrenees rising in the distance, the sun and flowers all about. The Miséricorde, a large orphanage and institution run by Catholic nuns, also fell under our survey with its crêche, baby clinic and refugee center. Besides these, the Americans met the nurses and midwives in charge of the clinics in Pau itself, carried under the auspices of the different branches of the French Red Cross. Then came the tabulation and the planned allocation of the milk, which was still on its way somewhere between the Spanish border and Pau.

At last, after a month of waiting, the milk really arrived and a committee met to make the final disposition of the gift: the two chiefs from the department, three French Red Cross presidents, a Belgian Red Cross representative, and the two American ladies. These people were happily surprised when they received answers to all their questions and had put before them the beautifully typed tables made as a result of the survey. A few changes were made, however, to take care of needs which had not been foreseen. For example, the Belgian Red Cross president asked for a supply of milk for the twenty-three babies being repatriated with a trainload of refugees, and enough milk for a seven-day trip was granted her. All the reckoning was based on figures by the Nestlé Company and after the supply was allocated it was found that 801 babies would be taken care of for a month, and that if the milk was used carefully the period might even be extended.

Then came the last chapter in this story: the ceremony of opening the railroad car and handing over the papers to the mayor. About twenty people were invited to come to the freight yard, and Martha Sharp made a beautiful little speech in French about the friendship of our two countries and the saving of these babies for France. When the mayor replied, his voice broke. After some pictures had been taken everyone went up the hill to the "foyer" for soldiers which the YMCA had organized and had a "vin d'honneur" in the approved French style, with the signing of names and more pictures. The Préfet, who is almost like the governor of one of our states, turned up covered with medals. If he had been on the stage, playing the part of a préfet, he would have been accused of overacting. He excused himself for not being able to attend the ceremony at the car, made a little speech, and kissed his wife. (He must have been so moved he had to kiss someone, and decided she was the safest.)

four

MARSEILLES

HAVING DECIDED TO REMAIN
and carry on what service was possible in France, I changed
employers. Instead of the North American YMCA, I now
joined the staff of the World's Alliance of YMCAs with
headquarters in Geneva. This body, based in neutral Switzerland, is mandated by international agreement for service to
war prisoners, and the agreement has been tacitly enlarged
to include service to civilian refugees. Since most of the
soldiers I had been serving were now being demobilized, no
further military service was needed. But southern France held
a dozen refugee camps it was now my duty to visit. Marseilles
was manifestly the vital center for all of unoccupied France,
and so a few weeks after my first visit, we moved to that
city, taking what we thought was temporary residence in the

Hotel Terminus at the St. Charles railroad station. As it turned
out, we lived there for two and a half years.

We found Marseilles a city teeming with refugees, Marseilles, which was already hundreds of years old when Pontius
Pilate came from Palestine to be its governor. The "Old Port"
harbored Greek ships at the time when Homer was writing,
and the fisherfolk up in the Greek quarter today use nautical
terms to be found in the *Iliad*. A town so maritime that its
streetcars had steamer horns instead of bells; its harbor dominated by the bright gold Notre Dame de la Garde, atop her
mountain, a guide to sailors for miles out on the Mediterranean.
The city's sun-drenched climate compensated somewhat for
its lack of a sewerage system. Like every other great international port city, Marseilles was normally a conglomerate of
all kinds of humanity, black, white and yellow, more than
six hundred thousand of them.

Just now the mixture was enriched by tens of thousands of
refugees. Although many of the million civilian refugees had
started the return to their homes, the streets were a kaleido-
scope of the military, already demobilized or simply lost in
southern France: colonials, with their bright red fezzes;
French Legionnaires, brown linen dust covers over their caps;
Zouaves swaggering along in baggy blue Turkish-style trou-
sers; men of the Chasseurs Alpins in olive green, their oversize
berets set so far over one ear they were almost slipping off
their heads. There were cavalry officers in their neat riding
breeches; black Senegalese, white turbans matching their ivory
teeth; tank corps men in padded leather helmets. They packed
the jolting streetcars; they overflowed the sidewalk cafés on
the Cannebière or the rue St. Charles. Many of these ex-
fighting men were as much prisoners in southern France as
any foreign refugee. Return to occupied territory would
make them prisoners of war immediately, and the Germans
forbade any able-bodied man to leave the country. Although
some more inventive souls had already found their way abroad,
the refined techniques of "export" for men who wanted to

join de Gaulle had not yet been perfected.

The city's alien population, crowding every available residence facility, was made up of men and women whose whole thought was centered on escape—escape by any sort of possible or impossible means. Every week there was a new decree limiting their freedom, and a consequent wave of panic that shook the whole spiritual atmosphere of the town. It was like an open pen of chickens with a hawk in the sky, circling ever lower. Like the camps, Marseilles seemed to live on rumor. It was reported that a ship en route from Senegal would bring great quantities of peanut oil and might take passengers away to some North African port. A Spanish refugee in Marseilles wrote to an American editor: "Our inexhaustible optimism is nourished by rumors that President Roosevelt has decided to send refugee boats, for which it appears the appropriations have already been voted. To the President we send this expression of our profound gratitude. But the boats must not delay. With each passing day our situation becomes more perilous. Only the young American nation can save us."

Like recurrent typhoons on a tropic island, every few weeks the rumor would sweep through the city: "The Germans will occupy southern France in a few days. Someone just in from Paris reported a concentration of troops at the demarcation line. It is said that the Palace Hotel is being cleared to make room for Nazi officers." As if to add credence to the gossip, one saw now and then a group of German officers in their long gray overcoats, their high turned-up peaked caps, their tall black boots with clicking iron heels, and their black gauntlet gloves—some "control commission" on business in the city.

Among all the milling refugees the most difficult problem was with those who had to get away and could not. For instance, here was Major Bredenbreucker: For the past four years he had been living in Paris, publishing venomous articles against Hitler and all he stood for. Well-known in the United States, within a few weeks after the debacle Bredenbreucker had a visa to go to America. All he needed was a French exit permit, then he could get the Spanish and Portuguese transit visas. But the application had to go to Vichy, and Vichy would send it to German headquarters at Wiesbaden and of course the Nazis would turn it down. They would then have Bredenbreucker's exact address, and soon after that they'd probably have him too. There were scores of men like him, marked on the Nazi "wanted" lists, active political fighters who had never given up and never were silenced by Hitler. Some of them were creative artists like Furtwanger or Leon Frank or Konrad Heiden. They all had the necessary emigration visas, but they were trapped in Marseilles, with their only way of escape some illegal method.

Some had paid boatmen to take them across to North Africa, or even just around the frontier line to a Spanish port, but the harbor was watched, of course. You might find a sympathetic harbor guard who would not look to closely at the documents a departing traveler carried, but you always risked being jailed and then, unless you could bribe your way out, the Nazis got you. And as for bribes, most of these people hadn't a sou. Some were even afraid to ask for relief, because this would reveal their addresses.

In Pau I had heard that there were guides who could be hired to take people over the mountains into Spain at night. The professional smugglers now did a business in human cargo. That was the case in Perpignan also, but a refugee had to be in good physical condition to stand the climbing, and some of our friends were afraid to risk it. Furthermore, one had to be sure the frontier guards had been "fixed." And then there was the 80 per cent chance the police on the Spanish side would put you in jail. It was fairly sure the Franco police had been supplied by the Germans with lists of men they were hunting.

All the southern French cities had scores of these marked men. Cities, because if they tried to live in a village where lodging was cheaper and food was easier to obtain, they would be as conspicuous as Breitscheid and Hilferding sitting on their café terrace in Marseilles. These two prominent German Socialists, both striking figures well known to the public, despite urgent warnings by their friends insisted upon spending most of every day on the terrace of one of the city's most popular cafés. They were political refugees, granted asylum in "free France," they insisted, and no one would dare touch them. This stubborn defiance of Hitler protected them for months, but one night they were both arrested and transferred to Germany. The vast majority of Frenchmen were anti-Nazi, especially in the villages, but some local gossip might give the refugees away, hence most preferred the cities.

Cigarettes at cafés were not the only item in short supply. Black marketeers were making small fortunes on essentials like oil and sugar. One day in Marseilles I tried a dozen shops before I could buy a small box of matches: matchbooks had long since disappeared from the market. "Scarcity" was the word on everyone's lips. Everything, it seemed, was rationed. Most of the space in the papers, reduced to a single sheet for lack of paper pulp, was given to articles on avoiding waste: how to keep vegetables from spoiling. France, which even at the end of World War I was still eating white bread, had by now almost forgotten what it looked like. Perhaps nothing reminded Frenchmen more of their fallen estate than the brownish, doughy mixture of substitutes for wheat flour, rye, bean meal—some said sawdust—they could buy with their bread ration cards. The papers told how a certain weed, properly treated, would produce a substance almost like sugar, how soybeans or sunflower seeds could be used as sources of oil. But all that was for next year, and most of the food stocks in southern France at the time of the armistice had gone to improve rations in Germany. The papers recommended that people gather a certain wild plant whose roots could yield a substitute for soap, while commenting on the difficulty of managing a household on the four ounces of soap per month now allowed by the rationing system.

In the cities the few taxis and still rarer private cars had to run on a mixture of alcohol and castor oil, the country's supply of gasoline being nearly exhausted. A few heavier vehicles had already been converted to charcoal or acetylene, and all left a most disagreeable odor behind them. Most of the makeshift apparatus was so bulky and generated such heat that it was unusable for passengers. With the disappearance of motors, traffic was in a bad way. Since most trucks were now museum pieces, everyone thought of horses. Appeal to the demobilizing cavalry brought out the information that all army horses had "gone north," like all the other movable supplies in the land. Failing horses, all kinds of means of locomotion had to be discovered. The bicycle became king of the highways, often equipped with a trailer for light deliveries. Pushcarts and other hand-drawn wagons, most of them hauled out of sheds where they had been collecting dust for twenty years or more, cluttered the roads. And as these rickety vehicles collapsed, one by one, they were abandoned by the roadside to accent the over-all picture of scarcity and disarray.

five

VICHY 1940
REVOLUTIONARY CHAOS

There had been refu-
gee camps in France ever since the collapse of the republican
army in the civil war in Spain, most of them hastily constructed
shelters near the Spanish frontier at either end of the Pyrenees.
Gurs, near Pau, and Argelès, near Perpignan, were typical of
these camps holding Spanish men, women and children, many
of whom had already been living in camps for two years
before the rout of the French armies in June, 1940.

When the exodus brought hundreds of thousands more
refugees into southern France, every available shelter was
pressed into service: some now disused military camps, schools
vacant for summer vacations, theaters, dance halls and cinemas.
These temporary refuges were gradually cleared, as their
residents moved to more normal housing, returned to their

homes in the north, or were moved into camps.

In September of 1940 the official estimate of the number of civilian internees was a hundred thousand. They were held in eighteen camps. Before the end of the year this number had been reduced to ten, not including some widely scattered small camps of foreign labor groups, at that moment only beginning to be formed.

Relief work in the camps before the French debacle had been carried on for about two years, by several agencies, French and foreign. The principal American organization involved was the American Friends Service Committee, already internationally known for service to those in distress regardless of political or national considerations. When the Germans occupied the northern half of France, all the various welfare organizations that, like the YMCA or the Joint Distribution Committee, had had headquarters in Paris, moved into "free" France, most of them to Marseilles.

To visit refugee camps I had to obtain official permits and passes. This motivated the first of a series of frequent visits to Vichy that I continued to make during the rest of my stay in France. The Minister of the Interior in Vichy controlled all the internment camps in southern France. This responsibility was natural for his department, whose prime function was command of the country's police force. Like other ministries in Vichy, this one exhibited a curious mixture of subservience to German orders and more or less secret sympathy with the Allied cause. Success in Vichy depended on the man you had to deal with, and whether or not he was willing to bear responsibility for any decision the Nazis might not like.

At first Vichy had reluctantly given permission to various relief organizations for work in the camps, but later a shift in the Pétain Cabinet brought into this office a man who perceived that in helping camp inmates these relief agencies were directly helping him with the many problems of health and control he found so difficult of solution. So when, as YMCA representative and arriving on the scene later than some others, I presented myself to this office, the Minister said: "Of course we'll give you permission—we know what your organization is doing for our prisoners of war in Germany."

Vichy in those days reminded me of Moscow in the spring of 1917, after the revolution. Grand hotels turned into offices and never swept since; improvised desks and other equipment in bedrooms now become offices, beds stacked with disordered files—everything with the tragically temporary air that follows the first days of revolution. In the Ministry of National Defense a group of soldiers, evidently part of the Ministry staff, lolled on the green velvet chairs in the lobby, dirty, unshaved, tunics unbuttoned. Most of the men over seventy who had formerly managed the affairs of France had been replaced by a lot of young fops with mincing steps and patent-leather hair, who could bow most respectfully and make sympathetic-sounding remarks to a visitor with a burning problem, but who were manifestly incapable of action of any sort, positive or negative.

This incapacity was due only in part to the character of the men themselves. When Marshal Pétain was leaving his post as French Ambassador in Madrid to become head of the French state, he said to friends there, "I am called to bury France." And just after the armistice he told newsmen, "The Germans hold us as in a vise." The whole apparatus of government of what Vichy insisted upon calling "Free France" was as impotent as an eighty-year-old paralytic.

The very external aspect of this world-renowned watering resort mirrored the painful situation. As autumn drew on, and it was impossible to fuel the heating plants of the luxury hotels where all the government offices were established, makeshift little wood-burning stoves began to appear in the rooms, stovepipes protruding from the windows. The only fuel available seemed to be freshly cut wood, and so all functionaries worked in an atmosphere as smoky as a campfire, while the brown creosote dripped into tin cans set under the pipes and all down the white stucco walls outside, leaving stains that would be there for years after the war was over.

The place was full of rumors. One day I learned "for certain" that the Germans were pressing Pétain to move his government back to Paris, threatening to set up another French government there themselves if he refused. The next day, it leaked out that a new shake-up in the Cabinet was imminent: the Nazis objected to having in the Cabinet a minister who was half Jewish. Prominent officials of the French Foreign Office or the Bibliothèque Nationale walked the Vichy streets, still stunned at being told "non-Aryans" were no longer wanted in Paris. Already a strong anti-Semitism was palpable in Pétain's government circles, soon evident in the new "Commissariat General for Jewish Questions" under one Xavier Vallat, who boasted to a German officer, "I am an anti-Semite of much older vintage than you." The yellow star of David that all Jews in occupied France were compelled to wear was not obligatory in unoccupied France. Someone remarked that this was one thing in which France refused to ape Germany, but a traditional anti-Semitism latent in France since the Dreyfus case, fed by writers like Maurras, had now become vocal. It was rumored that personally selected officials were scouring southern France to discover and list all Jews in government offices or other influential social positions.

Many thought "the Old Man," Pétain, was heading for a monarchy with a strong clerical reaction, although the *Journal Officiel* was still called the *Official Journal of the French Republic*. His proclamations began like those of the French kings: "We, Philip Pétain, Marshal of France, Chief of State . . ." New stamps and coins bore the Pétain portrait—not since the Second Empire had France seen the effigy of a living ruler on her coinage. A new law required that Pétain's portrait hang in every schoolroom. Pétain assumed the title held ex officio by the President of the French Republic, "Co-Prince of Andorra." Rumor had it that the Marshal had

become senile and that all decrees were actually issued by
the black-browed, heavy-jowled Laval, now almost supreme
in power. I once watched the old Marshal when he went out
for his evening stroll, alone save for a considerable group of
plainclothesmen. In civilian clothes he was not very conspicuous, and anyway at this hour all good Frenchmen were
at the dinner table, so there were few passersby to notice
him. He looked very weary and seemed to have difficulty
keeping his head erect. To journalists he gave his idea of the
ideal state:

"Parliament is undemocratic, true politics having for its
object the government of men . . . in conformity with their
highest interests. . . . Liberty can be experienced only under
a tutelary authority that must be respected and obeyed."

In another interview, not for French consumption, so
naturally published only in foreign papers, when asked about
the future of democracy in France, the Marshal explained
that if in postwar France there should be democracy (this to
be decided by a constituent assembly) it would not be like
what the country had known in the past, with all its frailties
and defects. One great advantage of a dictatorship, he said,
was its speed of action, unhindered by parliamentary discussions and divergencies of opinion. "In the future, all Frenchmen will think alike—with the young, this will be achieved
by education, with the old, by force."

The absence of a parliament, which so rejoiced the old
Marshal's heart, was often felt in the almost unending stream
of decree-laws issuing from Vichy. With no chance of having
a bill discussed from all sides before passage in Parliament,
it was not always easy to cover all phases of a topic in one
decree. Every day or two there would be new "explanatory"
decrees, setting forth that a certain new statute was not
intended to mean what it appeared to say, but rather something
else. For example, there was the decree ordering a general
census of all livestock, from geese and chickens to cattle, but
no one, in Vichy or elsewhere, could say just who was obli-

gated to count his stock—whether every family with a hencoop or a pig, subsisting leanly on kitchen refuse, or only large-scale stockowners.

Soon came the decree ordering all foreigners who had arrived in France since May 6 to report to the police or be interned, followed by a news item from Paris reporting mass raids on cafés, with hundreds of foreigners (read Jews) sent to concentration camps. The government instituted a "cour martiale" for the trial of Frenchmen who sympathized with de Gaulle, now coming to the fore in Britain. Trials of such persons must be held within forty-eight hours after the arrest, and the sentence executed within the two days following. The last previous cour martiale in France had been set up to suppress the Communist revolution of 1848.

Like most other Frenchmen at that moment, Pétain thought that Britain never could hold out against the increasing might of Hitler's armies. On several occasions he admonished the French that it was now time for a change of attitude: since Germany was evidently to be victorious in the war, one must learn to live with the Nazis, to cooperate in every way toward restoring the "real" France. Together with Laval, already named his successor, Pétain seemed to be aiming at some sort of French national socialism. Many French accepted this sage counsel, a few were already secretly in sympathy with de Gaulle, but most were too busy trying to restore their ruined businesses and find food, to trouble with political questions. At any rate, Berlin had announced that no disorder would be permitted, even in unoccupied territory, so the wisest attitude was just to go about the day's most pressing affairs and leave political thinking out of consideration.

A conversation I overheard in a government office in Vichy emphasized the complications of life in those post-armistice days. Here was a black-clad mother facing a sympathetic but helpless young officer at the information desk. The woman had been without news of her son since May—over four months—and after trying all sorts of other offices had finally appealed to headquarters. The officer could not hold out much hope. "You see," he explained, "that regiment was dissolved and all its records went to a depot. Now the depot has been abolished and no one knows what became of their files. If your son is in the occupied zone, he is a prisoner, and you will have to wait until the Germans send out a list containing his name."

Everywhere you turned, you encountered some new difficulty resulting from the division of France into two parts. Here was an officer of the General Staff who could not send a letter to his pregnant wife, left behind in Paris. Since no letters could pass the German line, he was in ignorance of her condition, with about as much chance of finding out as if she were on the moon. Some, rarely fortunate, had connections with the Red Cross, French or American, whose agents on infrequent occasions could cross the line, bringing news of kinfolk in the north. One by one the hundreds of railroad bridges destroyed in June were reopened, so that travel within the unoccupied zone became gradually more easy. But the demarcation line formed a barrier impassable for all but persons with extraordinary documentation.

The demarcation line bounded a territory that was the last refuge of some two hundred thousand people, French or alien, either having no place to which they might return or not daring to go back under Nazi occupation. France had been the last place of refuge for the political liberals and the Jews of all Europe. With more than half of France in the hands of the Nazis they had been fleeing, the other part became the last resort of these harried and helpless refugees.

For all of them Vichy held the only possible hope. Bumbling and makeshift as it was, it was still the government of France, and under a dictatorship it held the authority of life or death for "dirty foreigners." As months dragged on, the regime emphasized ever more strongly the distinction between French and aliens. Of the French, only suspected de Gaullists lived under such increasing pressure, but all foreigners had to place themselves under police surveillance. In an effort to get at citizens it disliked, Vichy ordered the reconsideration of all recent cases of naturalization, "to begin with the list of persons denounced as undesirable." If, after this procedure, one's passport was withdrawn—and a man without a passport was as helpless as an animal—one might appeal to a specially decreed commission, but the implication was that it would be uphill going to procure a valid travel document even for movement within the unoccupied zone. Even with his papers in order, anyone not a French citizen could not leave the village where he resided without a special permit signed by the prefect (governor) of the province, and a request for this permit often had to be referred to Vichy. This procedure guaranteed a delay of three to six weeks, by which time the reason for the journey had probably ceased to exist.

And beyond the limitations imposed on all foreigners were the special restrictions against the Jews, eventually including even those born in France and "more French than Napoleon." Replying to the rising protests of justice-loving men, French or otherwise, against this anti-Semitic legislation, the Vichy government issued its phenomenal statement of October 17 (1940), a sort of preface to Nazism in France:

"The texts already adopted by the Council of Ministers to regulate the situation of French Jews, or Jews resident in France, will shortly appear in the 'Journal Officiel.'

"In its task of national reconstruction the government has had, from the very first, to study the problem of Jews and of certain other foreigners who, abusing our hospitality, have contributed not a little to our defeat. . . . With certain quite honorable exceptions . . . the dominating influence of the Jews has made itself everywhere felt, especially in public services, leading finally to decomposition. All observers agree in affirming the evil effect of their activity in recent years, when they have had a preponderant influence in our affairs. These are the facts which direct the government's action in its pathetic task of French restoration.

"In its absolute serenity, the government has refused to undertake reprisals: it respects the person and the property of Jews: merely prevents them from assuming certain social functions, of authority, of management, of the formation of intelligence. Experience has proved to the government, as to all impartial minds, that Jews in these functions have exercised an individualistic tendency which has gone almost to anarchy. Our disaster imposes on us the task of regrouping French forces whose characteristics have been fixed by long heredity. This is not a matter of mass vengeance, but of indispensable security.

"The government may absolve from certain general restrictions prescribed in the national interest of France those Jews who deserve well of the fatherland, and this reservation proves in what a humane spirit it has set itself to regulate a problem whose universal character is demonstrated by our present disaster."

Most Jews could still not believe it, but for the wiser among them this unctuous declaration meant only one thing: escape from France as speedily as possible. Before long, helping people to escape from France was to be a principal part of my business.

six

GURS

Aᶠᵀᴱᴿ ɪ ʜᴀᴅ ᴍʏ ᴏꜰꜰɪ-
cial Vichy permissions I began my camp visits with Gurs.
During our first weeks in Pau after the exodus I had heard
dreadful rumors about this camp. Now I would see for myself.

After twenty miles on the bumpy little train southwest
from Pau to Oloron, the nearest railway station, I was lucky
to find a charcoal-burning taxi to take me the six miles by
country road and up the hill to the camp entrance.

In my service to war prisoners in Siberia in 1916 I had
visited many camps, and this one looked quite familiar from
the outside: two eight-foot barbed wire fences, fifteen feet
apart, with armed guards patrolling between the rows of
wire. Atop the fence at a dozen places were weather-beaten
wooden towers where watchmen were stationed at night.

The road side of the barbed-wire barrier stretched more than a mile along the roadway to Oloron. Outside, the nearest building to the camp was a dirty little café in a shack half a mile away.

Gurs was notorious long before this November day in 1940. The camp had been hastily constructed on a bare plateau south of Pau to harbor refugees streaming over the passes of the Pyrenees after the rout of the republican forces in the Spanish civil war in the spring of 1938. Built and originally managed by the French army, it was only later transferred to the charge of the Sécurité Nationale, the national police.

To the soldier at the gate (two buttons missing on his soiled horizon-blue uniform) I said that I wished to see the commandant. He stepped inside the gate and conferred with another guard, then motioned me to enter. The second soldier, rifle on shoulder, marched with me up the long central allée of the camp, delivering me at the shedlike office where some sort of secretary said the commandant would see me shortly, and would I wait outside? I sat on a bench beside the door and waited. Leaning against the wall beside me was a guard's bicycle, locked with a pair of handcuffs. Watching groups of ragged men slogging about in the muddy road, I could survey the camp.

A vast expanse of swampy plain in the shadow of the snowy Pyrenees, row after row of low wooden barracks sitting in a sea of mud. The soil was pure clay that the autumn rains had turned into a glutinous mass, almost impassable, except for the central roads and some narrow paths made of gravel from the river valley below. Built of uncured lumber, the windowless structures had never known paint, and the shrinkage of raw boards had left cracks which were stuffed with paper to keep out the wind. The trap doors in the roof were for ventilation, but they had to be closed whenever it rained, and then the only light was what filtered in from the single door at each end of the building.

The small city of eighteen thousand which was the camp

of Gurs was divided into ilots (sections) with a dozen barracks in each. Double rows of eight-foot barbed-wire fence separated the sections. No passage from ilot to ilot was allowed without permission from the commandant's office, so that those behind wire fences closely surrounding the buildings in each ilot were condemned to almost complete immobility. Guarded gates closed either end of the median "street." Even if outside the camp there was any place of refuge from the Vichy police, escape from here would be almost impossible.

A sea of mud: it had rained for days and the camp's brown clay soil had become a morass; it took tremendous effort to move any distance. If a man fell down, he was almost like an insect caught on flypaper—without someone to help, he could not get up. This was particularly painful for the thousands of old folk. The gravel paths leading to each barrack were negotiable, but all the surrounding earth was so sticky that for days on end refugees were confined to the dark and humid interior of the hutments. Another unintentional cruelty resulted from the fact that the crude shacks of latrines were set atop five steep and unrailed steps, risky enough for a sound-bodied man and especially treacherous for the hundreds of old people. The mud, the everlasting rain, the lack of beds and bedding, the scarce and insufficient camp fare—all helped to create dreariness and desolation.

The Spanish refugees, first inhabitants of Gurs, by now had little left in the way of clothing. Two years of camp fare had left them all as thin as sticks—poor legs and ankles so bony it hurt to look at them. The women were pitiful in their attempts to appear well dressed, most of them wearing galoshes or wooden sabots instead of shoes. Some of the very chic wore shiny rubber boots—the mud did not splash their stockings, if they had any. How some of them managed to procure make-up in this place of desolation was a mystery, perhaps explained by a remark I heard later about "camp-made prostitutes."

The commandant proved to be a smallish infantry lieutenant

named Bourdet. It is always the fate of refugees or prisoners of war to fall into the hands of second- (or third-) rate men: all the country's best are in active service somewhere else. Bourdet, for instance, had been an attendant at the city market scales, certain physical deficiencies having excused him from military duty. Further, these second-rate men come under extraordinary temptation: all purchasing, all supplies, involving sums of money a man had never dreamed of before, are completely in their hands. In one camp, one winter, most of the meager fuel allocation was sold on the black market, certainly with the connivance of the camp director. As in most other camps, here was little Monsieur Bourdet, in the position of God-omnipotent over the lives of eighteen thousand men and women, most of them more cultured, more capable, more intelligent than himself.

Bourdet received me politely, but with evident reserve. He examined the permission I had obtained in Vichy.

"You come from the Quakers?"

"No," I said, "from the YMCA," giving the name in French.

"Oh, yes—" he brightened visibly—"a friend of mine has just been released from a war prisoner camp in Germany (bad case of t.b.) and he told me about books your organization had sent to his camp."

"I hope we can do something like that here," I told him. "Does the camp have an orchestra?"

"Mon Dieu, no!" he said. "There's a little Jewish doctor here who plays a violin, but that's all."

"How about games like chess or dominoes—or a library?"

"You are perhaps connected with the International Red Cross also?" The Red Cross was the only organization with the right to inspect camp conditions, and the commandant was wary. I assured him I was not. "Our job is only with the cultural life in a camp," I explained, "but we can do much to keep folks in your camp busy with something more useful than complaining."

Now the commandant's defensive attitude began to soften.

"You are not bringing food or clothing? Look at those Spaniards out there."

"Our mandate is for nonmaterial help only," I explained, "as you will notice from the Vichy document."

"I see, and what do you want of me?"

"First your permission to find out what sort of things would be useful here. Is there a camp committee? Who could tell me, for instance, about the chance of building an orchestra? I can provide instruments."

"We don't allow committees," he said; then, turning to a clerk at a table behind him, "What's the name of that little man with the violin? You could talk with him," he told me; then, "Send a guard to bring him."

"I'd be glad to talk with the violinist," I said. "What about a library?"

"One of our guards here is a teacher in civilian life, and he has been lending a few books to inmates. Get Sergeant Fourier here too," he told the clerk.

While I waited I asked the commandant about religious services in the camp.

"Oh, we're well off," he told me. "There's a curé and a pastor who visit each ilot, and there's a rabbi among the internees. I've had them all watched and they seem reliable. Some of these Protestants, you know, are pretty far on the pink side. There aren't many Protestants here, anyway, and most of the International Brigade won't have anything to do with the curé."

At this moment Fourier appeared, and soon after the doctor-musician, violin in hand. The guard had misunderstood his instructions, and insisted that Dr. Weinberg present himself *with* violin at the commandant's office. Dr. Weinberg, a roundish man in his sixties, was somewhat breathless from the haste with which he had been haled to headquarters and from his sudden fear lest his violin be taken from him. Once he was reassured on this point he calmed down. The commandant sat in on our discussion.

Before I left I had the commandant's permission for Dr. Weinberg to study the orchestra question and prepare a list of instruments desirable. Sergeant Fourier was instructed to discuss the idea of a library in camp and to find out what teachers for what subjects might be available for possible educational classes. I made it clear to both men that I had no capacity for material relief of any sort and that I had no official connection with the administration, in Gurs or in Vichy.

By this time Commandant Bourdet seemed interested. He shook my hand cordially as I left and said the information I needed would be ready for me when I returned.

Ten days later I came to Gurs again: the same guard at the gate, the same procedure of a "planton" to accompany me to the commandant's office. This time Monsieur Bourdet was visibly upset.

"Look at this telegram, Monsieur Lowrie. I got it yesterday: 'Tomorrow you will receive two trainloads of German Jews. Make requisite arrangements.'—What do they think we are— miracle workers? Another three months, or maybe four, and this camp could be fit for habitation—that is, if Vichy would give us building materials. There's not a nail in this whole province, and even if you got permission to cut down trees and saw them into boards, where would you find gas for the machines? I'd hate to put my dog to live in most of these barracks—the lice would eat him alive. The Spanish have improved some of their ilots—after more than two years here, they've had the time. But what a headache they've been! Always quarreling among themselves about politics, bickering over personal problems!

"And where am I to discover beds for 'two trainloads of Jews,' I ask you? The Spaniards, of course, have the best sections of the camp, and most of them no longer sleep right on the ground, but with everything like straw sacks or even blankets requisitioned by the army, and since the armistice by the Germans—well, what does Vichy think we are, anyway?"

The commandant began to file his nails—it seemed to me
he was always filing his fingernails, especially since he "purchased" that silver-handled file from a Belgian refugee in
exchange for an extra bundle of straw for her bed. Perhaps
this operation was better than biting his nails; it seemed to
serve the same purpose, in times of stress.

"We laid ourselves out," he continued, "to get ready for
four thousand more Spanish internees transferred here from
Saint-Cyprien, and they were to arrive tomorrow. But I've
telephoned the commandant there to hold them until further
notice. He says they've broken up all their installations ready
for the move and they'll riot if they have to live any longer
in that lousy camp—but what can we offer them, any better?
Another month and we'll have some electric light, one bulb
to a barrack, and the worst of the leaking roofs repaired."

Even a man hardened to managing so primitive a detention
camp for nearly three years might now well be concerned.

The commandant invited me to go down to the station
with him. A small crowd of local people was watching a
stream of trucks drive up to the freight platform and move
off again. A heavy cordon of blue-uniformed soldiers kept
outsiders so far away that no one seemed to know for certain
what was happening. It appeared that these two trains had
brought German Jews from the Palatinate.

They stood on the station platform, crowded, cowed,
thousands of men, women and children. Many were gray-
haired, fine-looking, well-dressed people, some in fur coats—
apparently about an equal number of men and women. They
had come from Mannheim, Frankfurt, and other towns in
that area. Three days before, the Gestapo had knocked at
their doors and given them an hour, some half that time, to
prepare to go into exile. In the three days since then they
had never been outside their boxcars, and they arrived here
to be herded directly into trucks and hauled out to the camp.

You cannot imagine the misery: old, old women, fragile

and trembling; crippled old men helped along by younger women, all herded more or less gently by the French soldiers using a language these people from Germany could not understand. (Handling women and old people was something new for the army, and they did it badly.) Some had been taken from hospitals; some were feeble-minded. There were a few children, a few younger women, and the rest what you would find in any European city in wartime if you emptied every house and took away every resident: all the younger folk away at the front or in factories or in German concentration camps. Most of these newcomers were over sixty. Hundreds had been living in homes for the aged. The oldest member of the party was 106. No one knew why this particular group of eight thousand Jews had been suddenly picked up and shipped to that part of France that still called itself free.

The commandant had mobilized all the trucks available, some with tops and some without. Part of the time it rained, with a cold wind off the mountains. And here were these open trucks, jammed with helpless people squatting on their luggage or sitting on the edge of the box in the pelting rain, the baggage trucks behind also getting soaked. There was a larger amount of baggage than one would have thought, most of it good-looking, in ghastly contrast to the wretchedness toward which these people were bound. How quiet they all were! No chatter, no complaint. There was a tragic dignity about these exiles set down in a strange land, with no hope— if they but knew it—of anything in the future better than life in a camp like Gurs.

Watching this parade of suffering I noticed one woman who seemed to have taken charge of relations with the French for the whole convoy. Her erect bearing made her look taller than she was. She was wearing a sort of nurse's uniform, a gray dress under a dark-blue cape. She spoke excellent French, though with a strong German accent. Her amazing serenity and poise were in such sharp contrast to the confusion around her that the soldiers almost instinctively accepted her suggestions.

"If you could keep those four men together, it would be a good thing," I heard her say. "They are all from the same insane asylum." And then, "Could this woman and her baby go in the first transport? The child is seven months old, and the mother cannot nurse it, so it hasn't had milk for three days. I suppose we can have milk in whatever place we're going to."

Such a well-balanced person could give me a plain story of what had happened to these people: I asked the commandant's permission to ride in a truck with the newcomers, and climbed into the one with this self-possessed lady.

I found she preferred speaking German, and all the way to the camp we conversed about what had taken place. I learned that my new acquaintance had been directress of an old people's home in Mannheim.

"Four days ago, early in the morning," she told me, "the Gestapo came to us and told us to be ready in an hour for a long journey. Someone said something about France, but we did not believe it. You know how short of personnel all institutions in Germany have been. I do not yet understand how we managed to get all our forty old people dressed and ready. Most of them had suitcases or other travel equipment, and we packed what we could. When we got out in the street, there were two trucks, one with men in it, and the other with women and a few small children. In our home we had four old couples, besides three men without wives. All the men were put into the men's truck (how the women cried out!) but we thought we would all be going to one place. I have looked all through this crowd here and I cannot find one of these men. Monsieur, what do you suppose happened to them?"

It was only months later, and by roundabout ways, that I learned that these Mannheim men had been shipped directly to Poland and extermination. Now I said that perhaps there would be another train.

By this time Fräulein Sarah, as everyone was calling her, had discovered that I was not a camp official, not even French, but a welfare worker, and this gave her confidence. Her next remark struck me between the eyes.

"What kind of place is it, where we are being taken?"

What could I say? Gurs, with its mud and its smells and its lice! She had told me she had been a nurse in World War I.

"Well," I said, "you've probably seen some pretty dreadful situations. You will need all your courage and all your past experience to cope with this one."

Before we had time for more conversation, our truck rolled through the entrance gate of Gurs. Fräulein Sarah took one look at the barbed wire, the guards and the mud. As we got out of the truck, she seized my arm.

"Monsieur, this is terrible—and we are helpless. You must come to see me tomorrow.—Tomorrow, do you promise? You can see for yourself how we will need you."

I promised, and a soldier led her group away. It was getting dark, and I knew there was no use trying to do anything more that day. While I waited and watched the arriving trucks I began to wonder what I would do if I were suddenly thrust into a camp like this. I'd hope to have heavy, warm clothing and at least a blanket to sleep in. (At Argelès, another camp for Spanish refugees, they had never, in the past three years, had more than one blanket for every two men.) And I'd make up my mind at the outset to keep myself mentally employed: write so much a day, work on some sort of mental problem. The more I tried to imagine myself in this place the less I seemed able to think constructively. A sort of panic seized me, and I wanted to get away from there as soon as possible.

The commandant gave a garageman instructions to take me back to Pau on one of the empty trucks. But my anxiety to get away remained. I waited impatiently at the garage door for a truck to come up, almost climbed into one that had been ordered back to camp to haul straw for bedding, and had to wait ten minutes more for another. When I had got up beside the driver, to my horror he turned around and drove back to camp, the whole length of the main "street." Suppose the guard would not let me out? I had no exit pass, and I might suddenly be caught here like today's eight thousand newcomers. But no one stopped us, and I heaved a sigh as we drove out through the last row of barbed wire.

In Pau I had a lot of errands to do—I even discovered in one small shop two electric flashlights for use in those unlighted barracks—so I could not make the morning train for Oloron, and it was midafternoon when I reached Gurs and the commandant's office. And all at once I realized that I did not know Fräulein Sarah's family name. It would take hours to comb through the hastily prepared lists. By good fortune a clerk in the office recognized the person I was trying to describe. "Oh, yes, that woman—she's been helping with those crazy folk. She's in Women's Barrack Seventeen."

Here Monsieur Bourdet entered the conversation. "I think you should know this before you go into the camp. This morning another German mission (you know we're only eight kilometers from the demarcation line) came here and gave us orders about this shipment of Jews. The Germans will not tolerate any kind of soft treatment for these people, no good will on our part. For these folks no liberations are to be granted, not even if some have money enough to live outside. We know the Germans watch us pretty closely," he added, "but this is the first time they ever gave us orders like this. On one score they needn't have worried," he continued. "God knows we couldn't offer them comfort even if we wanted to."

I found Fräulein Sarah standing at the door of Barrack 17. The day was clear and the odor from inside seemed less offensive than usual. She held out her hand. I was surprised at the change in her appearance. She seemed to have aged overnight. There were dark circles beneath her eyes and in her expression something almost like terror.

"You were right," she said, with a grim nod toward the barrack. "It is the worst I ever saw, or dreamed of. With two insane women in this barrack, no one slept a wink all night. You know they took everyone from Mannheim, even from hospitals and insane asylums. One of the first things we must insist upon is taking our insane to some hospital or other institution."

I wondered what this morning's German commission would think of that.

"I was sure you would come," Fräulein Sarah went on, "and I've tried to get some sort of over-all picture of this section. You probably know that there are twenty barracks here. Some of them were already occupied when we came in to fill the rest yesterday. The word has got around that I'm a nurse, and I'm expected to solve all problems."

Here she was interrupted by a woman in a rumpled brown fur coat: "Fräulein, is it true that lice bites carry the plague?"

"No, it isn't true. Just don't worry about the lice. We'll try to get some disinfecting done soon."

"That's really the first thing we must arrange," she continued, turning to me, "that, and a supply of simple first-aid things and medicines. There's Frau Hiltz, who twisted an ankle last night when she tried to walk in the mud. And I've demanded a doctor for Fräulein Selig (once she was a contralto in the Berlin Opera). She's eighty and this noon she fell in the mud. I think it's a broken hip. You see, we've got all sorts of women here. Most of those in this barrack came from Düsseldorf. My Mannheim folks, the women, that is, are in barracks farther down this line. Next to me is Frau Samuels—she's a dentist, and next to her is a dressmaker's helper from Wuppertal. Oh, we've got to get a doctor here soon. I've used up all the small kit of bandages and medicine I brought with me."

I promised to speak to the commandant at once.

"There must be some terrible mistake, monsieur," Fräulein Sarah went on. "I know the French hate the Germans, but in a civilized country like France they would never permit bes-

tial treatment like this. As soon as word gets abroad about
what is happening in this camp, I'm sure we'll all be moved out
of here into some more decent place."

I tried to explain about the visit of the German commission
that morning, but without much success.

"And after medical care, what we need most is eating
utensils. In my bag I had a cup, and spoon, knife and fork, but
most of these poor people—today they had to eat with their
fingers out of a common dish, almost like pigs. It's incredible!"
Her voice almost broke. "Will you report this?"—and she
waved her hand toward the dark barrack interior. "There
must be a Jewish organization somewhere, or at least the Red
Cross—"

I promised, and hurried back to the commandant's office for
a date with the violinist. The two men had prepared a list of
instruments for a possible orchestra as well as data about textbooks and other reading material desired. I caught a ride on an
outgoing truck and went back to Pau.

I never saw Fräulein Sarah again. Those prisoners from
Saint-Cyprien that Commandant Bourdet had been expecting
were transferred to Gurs a few weeks later. And they brought
typhus with them. Until the epidemic had been stamped out,
no outsiders were permitted to enter the camp. I went back as
soon as it was possible. They told me Fräulein Sarah had volunteered for nursing duty in the Saint-Cyprien ilot and had
herself died of typhus.

seven

A MILLION OTHERS

A MILLION OTHERS, ALL OVER
Europe, were in camps more or less resembling Gurs, although
each had its own individuality.

There was that camp at Septfonds, northeast of Montauban.

There two thousand German Jews who had fought in the
French army were being held until someone, probably the
Nazis, decided what to do with them. Like all the soldiers of
the French army at the moment of the debacle, the only clothes
these people had were remnants of winter uniforms, after much
had been cast aside in the blistering summer heat. The commandant at Septfonds was very sympathetic and gave assurance he would do everything possible for "these brave friends
of France." With France under the German boot, most of
these "brave friends" ended their lives in the gas ovens in

Poland.

There was Argelès.

Like Gurs, Argelès was originally established to house the
remnants of the International Brigade of the Spanish civil war.
An agglomeration of flimsy, floorless hutments set on the broad
Mediterranean beach south of Perpignan, it held men of a
dozen nationalities. Not a tree, not a bit of grass. Like Gurs,
the place is tormented by icy winds from the mountains and
driving Sahara-like sandstorms. No artificial light, no heat and,
save in the women's section, no beds. Men had to sleep in the
sand, their only bedding the clothes they wore.

The one exception was a small sector where the working
parties lived. They might have beds if they could provide
them. And the result was motley, some beds consisting only of
a bit of cotton blanket tacked on a frame. One man who had
found a rusty sheet of corrugated iron roofing managed to
bend a foot of it down at right angles to the rest, tacked the
long end to the wall, and the short piece made a support at the
foot. This makeshift bed was only about four feet long, so that
its owner could not stretch out on it, but at least he did not
have to sleep on the vermin-infested sand. Some of these men
and women had been living at Argelès for two years or more.

The main street of the camp was a slightly wider stretch of
sand between rows of barracks. Every day thousands of men
strolled up and down here, with nothing to do. There were
two open-air barbershops; a sign which said "Chic Tailor,"
and another marked "Watchmaker" had arrows pointing to
barracks nearby. Men were selling and bartering all sorts of
possessions, their wares in their hands or spread on the ground.
One man had a half dozen "sandwiches"—slices of coarse gray
bread, each with a salt sardine on it. Several sold chestnuts;
their entire stock would have filled a quart jar. One displayed
a dozen tiny shriveled apples. Articles of used clothing were
being exchanged, shirts and socks and handkerchiefs; and there
was one "counter" with a dozen toy model airplanes, the only
item in the market representing anything but the most ele-

mentary utility.

On our first visit we were shown around Argelès by the fine Spaniard in charge, a smiling, fiftyish, very efficient man. He lived in his office, where he insisted on entertaining us at the end of our visit with "coffee" and small hard biscuits, which looked like our dog biscuits at home. The office was only one end of a dingy barrack, but it had a floor. The furniture consisted of a board nailed against the wall to make a table, and four stools, but the hospitality of this man was as gracious and genuine as if he were back in Washington, where, just a few years previously, he had been the Spanish military attaché.

In the women's sector were three thousand women, children and adolescent boys who did the camp chores. Here conditions were slightly better, because the barracks had floors, and rude benches served as beds. But when eighty to a hundred women and children are crowded into one room there is not much privacy. The American Friends Service Committee and a Swiss organization furnished a small quantity of milk daily for the younger children. There was also a children's school, housed in two small barracks at one edge of the camp, and a small sewing room, which provided occupation for twelve women (out of a thousand!). At the side of the camp next to the men's section a row of women sat in the sand, or stood against a ten-foot bank of barbed wire, talking to men leaning against the wire on the other side. In some ways such near contact was more terrible than if men and women had been in different prisons.

The camp director showed us a group of barracks devastated by recent floods. Here the camp garrison had lived. The barracks had floors, now covered by inches of mud. The Spanish leader had been given the job of clearing up this mess, and he and his men were doing it gladly, since they might be able to move into these better living quarters. Tons of mud were being dumped in a nearby field to make a kitchen garden.

The men only regretted that by moving they would have to leave their "library," constructed with great devotion in that

part of the camp where they were then living. They had lined
the low barrack with a lattice made of reeds from a nearby
swamp. The windows in this barrack were larger than those
in the ordinary barracks and the rafters and the railing around
the librarian's desk had been painted a warm red, the only
touch of color we saw in the whole camp. The leader proudly
told us that the entire expense for building this room was
twenty pounds of nails and six pounds of paint. There were
rude benches and tables and a blackboard, so that classes and
lectures could be held. I soon saw to it that the requisite materials were provided. The store of books consisted of a small
collection furnished by American relief organizations.

There was Vernet de l'Ariège, south of Toulouse, halfway
to the Spanish frontier.

The first time I was permitted to see anything of this camp,
except the office of the commandant, I was accompanied by an
officer and allowed to inspect the libraries we had installed
there, on the express condition that I speak to no one. Under
ordinary circumstances it might not have been so easy to
comply, but the atmosphere of fear and hatred in this camp
was such that, although I tried a score of times to convey a
greeting with my very friendliest smile, not one man responded with anything but a cold stare.

Another time, without realizing how it might frighten him,
I had a young fellow called to the commandant's office to put
into his hands a pair of glasses ordered especially for him. He
arrived in such a state of terror that at first he could scarcely
understand what I wanted him for.

Most of the camps in southern France were officially known
as "shelter centers": Vernet, on the other hand, was a "repression camp." It contained three categories of prisoners. The
first group consisted of a few hundred men who had difficulties
with the police, their offenses ranging all the way from first-
degree murder to failure to renew a passport on time. A
second group, slightly larger, consisted of "political extrem-
ists." The largest group was simply labeled "suspects." A

Vichy official sent to examine these cases told me that 70 per cent of the men had no idea why they were at Vernet.

Among the "suspects" was a man whose sons, born in France, had fought in the French army, where one was killed and the other wounded. Others had sons or brothers who fought with French forces as volunteers against Germany. There were men who had spent up to fifteen years in the Foreign Legion; there were men with the red ribbon of the Legion of Honor.

All this was immaterial in Vernet. What mattered was a bit of paper in the police files, some anonymous denunciation, unchecked or uncheckable. I knew of Belgians picked up at the border during the exodus and interned here, and Spaniards who had fled to France, never having set foot there before. The whole population of 1,600 was treated as though all were criminals, which entailed a regime of extreme severity.

The resultant distrust made it very difficult to initiate any YMCA work in Vernet. However, my persistent contacts with both camp management and some of the internees eventually made possible a fairly extensive program. Within a few months we had installed a library of 3,700 volumes in eight languages, which was widely used. The camp orchestra, one of our first successes at breaking through the watertight compartmentation within the great stockade, was permitted to give concerts in all three sections. Eventually we had twenty-six study groups, including courses in eight languages, accounting, chemistry and geology.

We provided the necessary equipment for a series of craft operations in which internees made games and wooden toys and furniture. Inspired by this example, a prisoner who had been the chief chemist at the well-known Coty perfume factory, proposed a Vernet soapmaking enterprise. This idea was accepted, and soon the shop, using mostly waste material from the camp itself, was turning out excellent toilet and shaving soap.

Being a prisoner in the camp at Vernet de l'Arriège was

quite different from internment in most of the camps. A friend of mine, Jules Levy, part-time correspondent for an American press agency, went through it.

As it happened, I was present when his experience began. Jules and I were at the censor's office one night, where both of us were filing cables to the States. This was a somewhat complicated procedure. One had first to get the censor's stamp on the text and then go halfway across the town to the post office to send the cable. In blacked-out Marseilles this could be a rather frightening experience. Just a few nights before, a man passing here had been robbed of all his clothes and left naked on the street.

We had gone down the narrow, smelly rue Colbert (open sewers always seemed more odorous at night) to a place where a blue-lit globe over a doorway marked the censor's office. The cramped little room had not been aired in years. And, as luck would have it, the man in charge was asleep. He came awake as Jules rapped on the little window, like a ticket seller's booth at a railway station, but he was in no pleasant mood. He scrutinized every line of the identity paper Jules handed him.

Jules had learned, as I had, that it was always best to show only one document at a time, otherwise the given official might become confused. "Is this all you have?" the censor kept grunting. And after a quarter hour of oppugnancy on the basis of the documents presented, he turned to the text of the cable. "How do you expect me to read English at this time of night?" and then, "Read it to me in French."

Like most educated Europeans, Levy's French was passable, although he had a better command of English. Off-the-cuff translating even from one's native language into a foreign tongue is not easy, while translation from one foreign language to another is apt to be easy only for professional interpreters at the United Nations. However, Jules stumbled through a French version of his cable. Probably nothing more quickly lowers a person in the esteem of any Frenchman, from the rector of the university down to a concierge in the fifteenth arrondissement, than imperfect use of the noble French tongue. Jules' French was like salt on a wound. "How do I know this is not full of some kind of double meaning?" the censor growled, at the same time affixing his faded purple rubber stamp to the paper. "I'll phone the post office to make you swear it isn't." After Levy had left, the censor telephoned the cable office: "There's an individual coming over with a cable in English—looks fishy to me. Better have him looked over."

The censor did not give me as tough treatment as he had Jules. After all, I had two A's in my favor: I was an American and Aryan. But the procedure took considerable time, and so I was not surprised, upon arriving at the cable office, to find that Jules had already left. I was to learn later that he never filed that cable. As he approached the post-office door, two policemen stopped him. At the police station he was searched and all his papers confiscated, despite his protests. Police questioning showed that there was no definite charge against Jules, but he was a foreigner, a Jew, and had connections abroad. "Probably a secret agent for the American consulate," one official said to another as they discussed the night's haul at the police station. "At any rate he's a suspicious character—belongs in Vernet. There's a whole section of suspects there."

That same night they started out. Jules had protested the seizure of his press card and had demanded permission to telephone the JDC office, without success. His would be just another of the sudden disappearances so frequent in Marseilles in those days. He was handcuffed to a frowsy Arab who, it appeared, had been caught picking pockets. Together with another manacled pair and accompanied by two militiamen with rifles slung over their shoulders and revolvers in holsters, they made the eighteen-hour journey to Vernet.

Jules had heard that the camps were enclosed by barbed wire, but save for border fortifications he had noted during World War I, he had never seen anything like Vernet. Two eight-foot wire fences, fifteen feet apart, and between them an entanglement of barbed wire which no one could dream of

passing without a cutter. Armed guards were patrolling outside, and Levy noted that all the guards inside carried revolvers. After the usual search of his pockets, he was assured
that their contents, including his identity papers, would be
held for him in the office, and while his Arab traveling com-
panion went off to one section of the camp, Jules was put into
the "political" area.

When he got back to Marseilles he told me the story: "My
first impression was shock and almost horror as I faced the
others there. How could men be held in such conditions? They
looked like walking corpses. I knew food was scarce in France,
but we were not yet starving. In my ordinary decent street
clothes, I felt like a show-window mannequin: these men
were wearing what was left of the clothes they were arrested
in, two or three years before. Someone showed me a place on
the sleeping bench where I could crowd myself in. Some of
the men had blankets, but I found the smelly barrack so hot I
thought I wouldn't need one: before morning I felt differ-
ently. Someone also gave me a large sardine can that was my
sole eating equipment for days, until I could find another
internee who sold me a spoon. We ate standing: there were
no tables, and the only place to sit was the edge of the lower
tier of bunks. And there was only cold water to rinse out our
tin cans after we had eaten. I met one young student there
who had a rough tabouret. He said it had saved his reason. He
could take the stool and go into the farthest corner of the
barbed-wire enclosure, turn his back to the crowd, and sit
there and read. Someone had given him a Bible, and in four
months he had read it from cover to cover.

"After a few days I got used to the smell, and learned to
leap to 'attention' every time the adjutant came into the
barrack. These hutments had been built in summer, of un-
seasoned boards, and the weather howled through every crack.
But the cold was not as bad as the bedbugs. Although you
could buy some sort of insecticide at the canteen, it seemed
impossible to keep the bunks clean. At the canteen you could

also buy writing paper and candy. One political from Lyon complained that he could not buy butter or bacon, and couldn't believe me when I said we hadn't seen these in Marseilles in months.

"There were a lot of Germans, and even Italian Jews, in our section of Vernet, men for whom not the French but the enemy had the last word. In all the time they had been there, no one had been presented with any accusation or been given any reason why he was shut up in the place.

"What did we do to pass the time? Mostly we read. Your YMCA library was a lifesaver. Incidentally, the librarian had had a Paraguayan visa waiting for him for sixteen months, and still could not get permission to go to Marseilles to pick it up and so escape from France. Then there were gramophone concerts. They were really the only contact with the world outside that most of us had.

"Of course there were interesting people one could talk with. One very notable man carried himself like a German officer. He was an ex-member of the Prussian Landtag who moved to Paris after Hitler took over. There he was secretary of a Socialist party, and was arrested the night war was declared. He has no hope of leaving Vernet until the war is over. Unless, of course, a Nazi commission finds him. He's registered under a false name, but someone might recognize him—he stands out above the crowd like an old tree. Another chap had what he claimed was a complete list of all relief agencies in France, and some in America. This he would rent out to anyone with money to pay for it."

Levy was one of the few men I knew of who managed to get himself released from Vernet. We knew he had excellent connections at the American consulate, but we never asked whether they had intervened on his behalf.

eight

THE NÎMES COMMITTEE

WITH THE YMCA OFFICE ES-
tablished in Marseilles, I began contacts with various agencies
working in camps. Already a score of organizations were
engaged in helping refugees, in or out of camps, but I soon
discovered that in general each was working in its own spe-
cialized field, with quite insufficient knowledge of what others
were doing. So I began a series of calls on the principal
agencies, suggesting some better coordination of our efforts.

There was an almost comic element in my taking this initiative. Although I was now officially working under the World's
YMCA in Geneva, and had a gold-sealed document attesting
to the fact, and although Geneva had assigned a budget for
our work, that office had neglected to send me any money or
even inform me that funds were available. Now, I couldn't

provide libraries and orchestras for a dozen camps on the small amount of relief funds left in our cash box after the expenditures for the soldiers' club and a children's château in Pau and considerable general relief. Here I was, representing a world organization, with almost no money to start my work. I had to think of some useful service that would cost nothing. I had first broached my idea in Vichy.

To my question, "Would you think it useful to attempt to coordinate the work of these agencies?" the Minister of the Interior replied: "What an excellent idea! Why don't you do it? You have my official request, and my backing for whatever you can work out."

This was the origin of the "Coordination Committee for Relief Work in Interment Camps," soon to become known across all of southern France as the "Nîmes Committee," because the lovely Old Roman city of Nîmes, near the geographic center of the score of relief agencies at work in camps, was the site of the Committee's monthly meetings. The idea of a coordinating organ for unofficial groups (the later term was NGO for Non-Governmental Organizations) was readily accepted by almost all the agencies. Someone remarked to me at the time: "If you can coordinate the Quakers you will accomplish something no one has ever done yet," but I have to record that no other organization collaborated more wholeheartedly with the Committee throughout the whole of its existence.

On November 5, 1940, we held a small preparatory meeting at Quaker headquarters in Toulouse, and on the 20th the first organization meeting took place in Nîmes. Officers were elected and I was chosen chairman, a position I held until German occupation of southern France forced me to move to Switzerland. One meeting of the Committee was held after that, but regular operation under the Germans was manifestly impossible, and the removal to interment in Baden-Baden of many of its members practically closed the Committee's history.

At our first meeting we agreed that monthly meetings would be held, and we chose an executive committee among organizations stationed in Marseilles to take any interim action necessary.

I do not recall that the Committee ever had a treasurer, or even a budget. The YMCA office in Marseilles was chosen as headquarters, and was to take care of all the necessary clerical work: circulation of minutes and reports or other Committee business. By this time I had received funds from Geneva and could comfortably offer this service.

Our first meeting set the tone for cordial and complete cooperation that never failed throughout the Committee's life. As I opened that initial session I glanced at the alert faces around the long table. What a gamut of nationalities and interests they represented! Of the twenty-five member agencies of the Committee that day, five were world organizations, a dozen others were national, like the American Friends of Czechoslovakia, the American Joint Distribution Committee, the American Friends Service Committee, the "Belgian Office" or the Swiss Aid for Children. Some were religious, some not, such as the French Red Cross or the International Migration Service.

Besides those just named, we had the Polish Red Cross and YMCA, the French YMCA and YWCA, two instances of joint representation, the French Student Christian Association, the Unitarian Service Committee, The World's Alliance of YMCAs, the French Committee in Aid of Jewish Refugees, ORT (Jewish technical education organization), OSE (Jewish children's relief agency), the European Student Relief, the Central Jewish Committee of Relief Organizations, the French Protestant Federation, the CIMADE, a joint relief agency of French Protestant youth organizations, HICEM, the Jewish emigration society, RELICO, a Jewish organization for health and medical service, the Catholic Centre d'Accueil, and a personal delegate of Cardinal Gerlier.

For many agencies, less well known to French officialdom

than the YMCA or the International Migration Service, membership in the Committee gave official recognition and approval of their work. The Polish Red Cross, for instance, at a time when Poland no longer existed so far as official France was concerned, was enabled to continue its efforts on behalf of the thousands of Polish refugees almost until the German occupation of the whole of France. The Belgian Office, a sort of combined Red Cross and unofficial consular service, came under the Nîmes Committee umbrella, whereas the Nazis, had they been consulted, would never have permitted any Belgian organization to exist.

Even purely French organizations, by the very fact of their existence only in unoccupied France, were in spirit anti-Nazi, and hence suspect by the German-controlled government in Vichy. It was not strange that the Vichy Secretary of State called the European Fund for Student Relief, "Fond Européen de Secours aux Etudiants," the "Front for Student Relief." And with the steadily increasing anti-Semitic pressures in Vichy, Jewish organizations in particular needed coverage and protection.

One of the outstanding achievements of the Nîmes Committee was the complete and sympathetic collaboration of Christians and Jews. The majority of all refugees, inmates of internment camps or living outside, were Jews, but of the twenty-five organizations meeting in Nîmes only six were Jewish. Despite religious differences, the services coordinated by the Nîmes Committee were available to all refugees, without distinction. And in frequent cases where it seemed diplomatic for a Jewish organization not to appear in the picture, some special project would be turned over for execution to the French Protestant CIMADE or to the Quakers, the Jews simply providing the necessary funds.

As the anti-Semitic influence in Vichy became more dominant, there were frequent instances where Jewish organizations working alone were refused permission for new projects but where collaboration in the Committee made these possible.

Our presentation and recommendation of these programs often secured the necessary authorization.

Then, although the Nîmes Committee sedulously avoided politics, the overriding sympathy of all its members was wholeheartedly with the Allied cause, and a spirit of mutual confidence developed which was one of the most gratifying elements in its operation. This fact of both organizational and spiritual unity gave the Committee, with all its international connections, a prestige and influence with French authorities that proved to be of even more significance than coordination of effort. Coordination was achieved, the tasks of each organization defined, information shared and resources pooled, and from the purely functional viewpoint the Committee would have amply justified itself. But with no primary intention of so doing, it also became the sole defender of the interests of a hundred thousand otherwise defenseless refugees. All these helpless people, German Socialists, Poles or Belgians for instance, were officially or *de facto* stateless. No consular or other governmental office existed to concern itself with their affairs, to aid in such legal procedures as visas and emigration or to protest mounting injustices culminating in deportation to the extermination camps in Poland. So, soon after its inception, the Comité de Nîmes found that it could—and must—speak with one voice to Nazi-dominated officialdom, and found also that in most cases it would be heard. As a matter of fact, within a few months after the Committee began to function ministers in Vichy, realizing how much the various relief agencies could ease their own tasks, began presenting problems to the Committee, instead of vice versa. On one occasion Vichy requested that organizations in the Committee, established officially for aid to refugees, extend their services to camps where French citizens were interned.

Happily, most of the Committee's relations with Vichy were not in the form of protests. By viewing the situation from the internees' standpoint and collecting data on one or another problem, the Committee was often able to present possible solutions and even to propose cooperative effort by government and private agencies. Such suggestions were usually accepted by Vichy. One worker wrote after a Nîmes Committee meeting: "The acceptance of these propositions will practically revolutionize the lives of sixty thousand unfortunate people in camps."

Soon the Committee's meetings came to be the high points in the lives of relief workers in Vichy France. Morning trains from east and west arrived at Nîmes at about the same hour, and all-day meetings in the comfortable Hôtel Impérator could begin by 10:00 A.M., finishing late in the afternoon. The noonday luncheon, perhaps only because of the company, always seemed a bit more appetizing than the sometimes strange fare served in most French restaurants, all operating under near-famine conditions.

At a meeting the group around the long table might include from twenty-five to forty persons, of the most varied types. There was Abbé G. of Jewish origin, now one of the leading Catholic social workers in France. Among the official representatives of the *American* Friends Service Committee were a Danish lady and a Russian princess; there was a former ambassador and an ex-consul general. The representatives of Jewish organizations were equally varied. There was a young American, baffled and frightened by his first experience in a strange country and still more by the anti-Semitic atmosphere in which he had to work, yet with no idea of retiring, as he might have, to safer and more normal Lisbon; there was also one of the outstanding authorities on jurisprudence of imperial St. Petersburg, a gray-bearded veteran of many battles for social justice. Like this man, several other Committee members were experienced in relief work during World War I and later. There was usually a visitor officially permitted to come from occupied France, like the charming and courageous Madame Chevalley of the International Migration Service, who brought news from the other side of the demarcation line. Sometimes one or more representatives of some

Vichy ministry were present, and on one occasion the Inspector General of Camps himself.

What did we discuss in these monthly meetings at Nîmes?
Everything concerning the lives and conditions of refugees,
in camps or outside, even on occasion those outside metro-
politan France, as when we dealt with refugee situations in
Colomb-Béchar or Casablanca. We always had a general survey of the state of affairs in various camps, changes in administration or legislation concerning refugees, and a report of
what each organization had been doing during the past month.
As time went on and the agencies became more closely acquainted, the number of joint projects constantly increased:
the Jews or the Quakers would open a home for children, the
Unitarians would provide medicines or educational personnel,
and the YMCA the library, with the French Red Cross
responsible for legal arrangements and permissions from
Vichy. With constant changes of personnel in the ministries
and what seemed like perpetual movement of refugees from
one camp to another or even the closure of certain camps
resulting in part from pressure by our Committee, at each
monthly session we faced new conditions and had to adjust
to altered situations. At one meeting, for instance, I could report that our proposal for opening a new camp for internees
over sixty had been accepted, and at the next we assigned to
Committee members the different tasks of equipment, health
and cultural services in the new location.

Some items from the minutes of a meeting in October, 1941,
are illustrative of our work. All Committee records were
seized by the Germans when they occupied Marseilles, but
for some reason this report survived. "The transfer of children
from Argelès to Rivesaltes is practically complete." (The first
groups were transferred without any preparatory disinfection
precautions, so they took with them to a comparatively clean
camp all the filth and illnesses from Argelès.) "Despite the
rude climate, the fleas and the rats, Rivesaltes is preferable
to the degrading atmosphere of Argelès. It will be necessary

to check on feeding. The American Red Cross is asked to provide supplementary food for the children.

"New measures of 'recruitment' for the foreign labor groups are discussed. Thousands of refugees living in towns on state subsidies, including men ill with t.b., have been taken. The Committee Chairman is asked to intercede with Vichy, especially for students, some of whom have been removed just before their examinations.

"The new apprentice school planned by the ORT organization has not been opened because the authorities requisitioned the premises already rented for that purpose. Other buildings are being sought. But the apprentice courses in Rivesaltes are already functioning."

Another minute reports that an exhibit of handicraft by the inhabitants of Gurs had just been held. "It was most successful, but how are we to sell the products without risking damage to the national economy of France?

"The delegate of Cardinal Gerlier reports that three hundred Catholics, former German and Austrian citizens, are to emigrate to Ecuador. He hopes this will create a precedent, and that many others may escape by this method.

"Some organizations are having difficulty with permission to enter some camps. A circular issued at our request by the Prefecture at Marseilles has not had the effect desired. It is decided that the Chairman will present a complete list of representatives of all our agencies and secure block permits on his next trip to Vichy."

Thanks to the complete cooperation of the Committee members and our avoidance of political discussions, the Nîmes Committee quickly acquired status and influence which its members individually could never have had. As its chairman, I was able to meet with anyone in Vichy we thought it useful to interview.

Money came to us in various ways, legal and illegal, mostly the latter. As a matter of fact, I did not always understand the processes myself. One day in Marseilles a man I had never

seen before came into my office "with a message from Mr.
Marshall." Mr. Marshall was an American businessman whose
acquaintance I had made on one of my trips to Vichy, and
with whom I had once discussed the problem of money transfers. I had not seen him for weeks. Now here was his message:
"Mr. Marshall thinks it would be good if you were in a room
in the Hôtel Terminus in Lyon between twelve and two next
Wednesday." Looking up railroad schedules, I found there
was a good train from Marseilles that would land me in Lyon
shortly before noon, and that another left Lyon at 2:10 for
Marseilles. Although I was a regular client of the Hôtel
Terminus, which is a part of the Lyon railroad station, and
could always count on being lodged there, somehow, I took
no chances on this occasion and wired for a reservation several
days ahead.

My room was ready when I reached Lyon and from noon
on I dutifully waited to see what would happen. An hour
passed. Then the telephone rang, but it was a call for a Monsieur de Couderque, either someone who had recently occupied this room or perhaps an error by the hotel telephone
operator. The lady begged my pardon. One-fifteen, and still
nothing happened. I had read from beginning to end every
paper I had brought with me; newspapers were slim things at
best in those days of paper shortage. French hotels never having
heard of the Gideons, there was nothing else in that room to
read, and if I left the room long enough to buy more reading
matter on the station platform, that might be the moment
my expected visitor would arrive. Nothing to do but pace
the floor. A quarter before two, and still no sign of action:
was the whole thing a mistake? Had something happened to—
whom? I was closing the small suitcase I had brought, when
at five minutes before two there was a knock at my door. I
opened it to a stranger, who entered, gave me a quick looking
over and asked, "You are Mr. Lowrie?" I nodded. Without
further word the man handed me a parcel about the size of a
paving brick wrapped in newspaper, and turned to leave.

"Don't miss your train," he reminded me, as he was closing the door on his way out. Stuffing the package into my suitcase, I ran for my train. No receipt of any kind was asked or given. Back in my Marseilles office I opened the parcel: it contained a million five hundred thousand francs in beautiful, new one thousand france banknotes. Even at the then fallen rate of exchange, this represented five thousand real dollars. I knew this transaction was the result of that one conversation in Vichy about exchange, but what and who had come between then and my receipt of the money, I do not know to this day.

Usually under-the-counter exchange operations were not quite so mysterious, although they always had to be secret. We had a code expression for these transactions: "the available balance." Sometimes in a conversation you would be given the name of a man who possessed francs; you went to see him, and the arrangement was made. Sometimes an organization—the Polish Red Cross for example—had an exchange arrangement they kindly shared with others. For a considerable time one perfectly legal method of obtaining a better than official exchange rate was to turn dollars into French francs in Switzerland, and bring the currency into France: while you had to declare the amount you were carrying, there was no legal limit to the sum you might be transporting. But, as one of my reports to New York headquarters, written from outside France, reads, "the 'available balance' system works smoothly and gives better results than can be had in Switzerland." The same report continued: "I am cabling you today to deposit five thousand dollars as the last time . . . As regards further operations, you will have to trust us and make deposits where and as we request."

There were rare men—the secretary of the Reformed Church at N., an anonymous Venezuelan in Lyon, and Monsieur Bernard, devoted French patriot later shot by the Germans—who managed more or less regularly to cross the line of demarcation, sometimes smuggling in packets of French banknotes, with instructions as to where the equivalent dollars were to be deposited in the States or in Berne.

Monsieur Bernard seemed to have a special guardian angel, for he crossed the line about once a month and was never apprehended by the German police until southern France was occupied. When he was finally arrested, a Frenchman and fellow patriot, not a German, was responsible. Bernard had called on a wealthy industrialist in his home in Lyon to arrange for an unusually large transfer of funds. As was not at all unusual, the two men had met for the first time. When Bernard was leaving, the valet, handing him his overcoat, noticed that it had been purchased in Vienna. He immediately suspected that Bernard was a provocateur, sent by the Germans to trap the industrialist. Here was a tragic predicament. The industrialist could believe Bernard was who he claimed to be, and carry through the arrangement, involving no small risk, as they both knew. But suppose he was a German agent? In that case, the only way for the industrialist to avoid arrest and almost certain death would be to report at once that Bernard had approached him. If, on the other hand, Bernard was honest, reporting him would deliver a fellow patriot to Nazi executioners. After anxious consideration, it was decided to inform the Gestapo, and when Bernard called the second time, as agreed, they were waiting for him.

Of course these complicated and clandestine exchange operations could get out of hand. With almost no written records, no one's memory could be infallible, and sometimes something other than perfect order prevailed. The experience of one prominent member of our Nîmes Committee in this connection is illustrative. Like all the rest of us, he was concerned with a number of different operations: supporting persons and organizations aiding Jewish refugees to escape, financing part of the French underground, as well as carrying out the nominal work of his own organization. This man had not had much experience in financial matters, and out of need he began to use what funds he happened to have on hand for one or another of his projects without too much regard for the actual designation of the money. No one ever doubted his absolute honesty, but matters became so complicated that, once the war was over and attempts to bring financial order out of chaos had proved hopeless, his sketchy records were simply destroyed, all concerned agreeing that the man had done an excellent job. After all, it was part of the common cause.

Occasionally in the money business we encountered peril from within our own ranks. The pastor who was one of the vice-presidents of the Nîmes Committee left his briefcase, containing some financial and other papers of a thoroughly "classified" nature, in a train. Although, in consequence, his home was ransacked by the police, no one of our other organizations suffered the special police attention we expected. Another time our YMCA cashier in Geneva, as unimaginative as he was honest, sent me via open post some monthly accounts including details on certain "available balance" transactions. Again, as by a miracle, this letter seemed to have been unopened by censors.

There were occasions when gray-market financial arrangements were accepted by officialdom itself. At one moment a certain Czechoslovak we suspected of Nazi leanings, who seemed to have undue influence in Vichy, tried to persuade the government to liquidate the Czech Aid and appoint a special French committee to take over our work. By some clever negotiating in Vichy, our men were able to reach an agreement and form a small committee, under the patronage of the Ministry of Foreign Affairs, that would administer relief to Czechoslovaks. To this committee we referred a score of names that could be sent to Vichy without danger to the persons themselves, while continuing—without saying so aloud—all the rest of our Czech Aid operations as before. It was agreed that I, as president of the Czech Aid, would send twenty thousand francs per month to the new committee. Consequently, I received a letter from the Vichy Foreign Office instructing me to transmit French francs in banknotes to the new committee, via the French Consul General in Geneva. Such transmission of banknotes, purchasable in Switzerland at a third of the official exchange rate, was by this time illegal, but I could soon show an official receipt for my first official black-market transaction.

Of course we had no bank accounts. Some of the organizations had office safes where currency could be kept. Our improvised YMCA office in Marseilles had none, so most of the time our entire capital was stored in a suitcase under the bed in our hotel room. There were times when this treasure amounted to more than a million francs.

Another financial headache affecting most of our relief agencies was the matter of transferring funds to individuals near us, in camps or outside. Sometimes money would come from a New York or a Lisbon office, the amount indicated in dollars: "Transmit to Hans Schelling $10.00." Now at what rate of exchange should we pay Hans Schelling the ten dollars his brother in New York was sending him—at the legal rate or something three times as good? If Schelling chanced to tell the wrong person that he had received an "extralegal" rate, that might get us into trouble: if he was normally intelligent he would know the common gossip among refugees about gray-market rates, and so might reasonably expect us to use this figure in paying out his brother's transfer. We all decided to make individual transfers only at the legal exchange rates. This was sure to cause criticism among refugees, but it was safer for all concerned.

Even if we remained completely within legality, transfers to individuals brought frequent difficulties with the police. Sometimes requests for transmission to individuals came from an organization like the British Red Cross: there would be a list of names with no indication of the identity of the individual senders. Some British licenses forbade the agency to reveal the senders' names. In one such case the Quakers had an unpleasant time with the police because they had transmitted a considerable sum to the wife of an officer known to be with de Gaulle. Another agency received a list of persons, each of whom was to receive the same amount. All of these men were known to be politically suspect, and again the police came inquiring. Since it was not the function of a transmitting agency to investigate the political loyalties of a person to whom money was sent, any more than the use to which it was put, the situation was awkward in the extreme. One of the largest American organizations in Marseilles was quite sure that it was being used to "contribute to the support in France of the dependents of many persons in the Free French forces abroad." But the recipients would otherwise have been destitute, so transfers continued until the German occupation.

Receiving money from abroad was one thing; delivery was quite another. Six months might elapse between Solly Kahan's appeal to a relative in New York and the arrival of an answering check. In that time Kahan had probably left the camp from which he first wrote, might have lived somewhere outside for a while, been reinterned (because the check had not reached him and he was again penniless), or perhaps was in hiding. When the German occupation closed all our agencies, the undelivered "transit" amounts totaled several million francs. However, French citizens left in charge of American offices succeeded in distributing the greater part of these funds to their destinations. The remainder soon became valueless through wartime inflation.

nine

EMIGRATION

MIGRATION WAS THE WORD ON
everyone's lips. At first this meant quite legal procedures,
with visas and exit permits: later it signified escape by any
possible method, legal or not. In the case of the thousands of
refugees living in freedom in unoccupied territory, the Nazis
could do nothing to prevent their further movement, or so
it was thought. But cases were all too frequent of persons
the Nazis wanted to seize, such as German Socialists, arrested
by the Vichy police and last heard of in German prisons.

For the refugees in camps who had some legitimate hope
of emigration, the situation at first was maddening. One of
the armistice conditions provided that the French must return
to German hands any German citizens, present or past, whom
the enemy indicated they wanted. So until German commis-

sions could visit each camp (thanks to sympathetic French officials in most camps, they found few of their sought-for prey) no departures were permitted.

Then toward autumn (1940) the authorities came to a realization of the problem posed by the further presence in the country of thousands of "exportable" persons. Unwanted in France, forbidden to earn a living, there had been no place for these people save the camps. But with famine threatening as winter approached, there was suddenly a great dither about hastening the departure of anyone with a valid travel permit, and all the Nîmes organizations were pressed to do their utmost to expedite emigration, before winter if possible. The Committee had records of over two thousand persons who claimed to be in possession of all the necessary documents, and this enabled speedy action. Two of the agencies, specialists in emigration operations, had to carry the brunt of this sudden "export" effort. Others aided in every possible way: taking census in camps, interviewing and registering applicants for travel abroad, and intervening with authorities, local or national, for the almost endless series of documents required for each prospective traveler.

Even then a refugee found it no simple matter to get out of camp, which he had to do, to obtain any sort of papers. A Vichy decree stated that anyone who could prove admissibility to a foreign country, presenting either a visa or the justifiable hope of securing one, could be transferred to the "transition camp" at Les Milles, near Marseilles, where all the consular and other related offices were located. "Could be," "if they have sufficient means to make the trip." And in the early months, for a penniless internee in Gurs, for instance, hundreds of miles from Marseilles, the decree was merely a new source of torment. The one terrible exception to this generous ruling of Vichy was with regard to former German and Austrian citizens. They were not permitted to travel anywhere until each case had been passed upon by the Vichy—which meant Nazi—police. If they were returned to German hands, it would mean torture or death or both.

In the matter of emigration it soon became evident that, though many called, few would be chosen. In the autumn of 1940 we all thought that orphans, at least, might be easily emigrable. We even hoped that other children and their mothers might have permission to travel abroad. With few exceptions refugee families had been held together. Mothers and their children were placed in the same camps: the fathers were probably away in some "foreign workers' group" building a sea wall on the Atlantic coast, under British aerial bombing, or working in factories, French or German, farther north.

Hundreds of youngsters had kinfolk in the United States, sacred goal of almost all would-be emigrants, and soon the requisite affidavits began to reach Marseilles. "Affidavit" became a word as international as "emigration." Generally it was pronounced "ahf-fee-dah'-veet," but anyone knew what it meant.

An affidavit, however, was only the first difficulty. With this in hand a HICEM agent, or a representative of the International Migration Service, could undertake securing French permission for the actual departure, but only after the document from America had been personally presented to the United States consul in Marseilles and he had studied it. In some cases he passed it on to Washington for decision. After all this, three or four foreign visas had to be procured and passage by rail and steamer assured. And the time all this required! And the risk and expense! For a refugee, the difficulties were almost insurmountable. How do you manage to take yourself and your family from some small village near Pau, for example, all the way across the country to Marseilles on the chance that your American document will be found acceptable?

For illustration, take the "Unitarian Children's Group" as we called it. Shortly after the fall of France the American Committee for the Care of European Children had the admirable idea of bringing a group of French children to the States "for the duration." Many British children were being received in American homes, and were thus assured of normal living while their own homes were experiencing Nazi bombs. The Unitarian Service Committee agreed to have Martha Sharp represent the American Committee. So she came on to Marseilles after the milk distribution in Pau was finished, to work on the new project. She was installed in one corner of our YMCA office. For a rug to cover the stone floor, the only thing purchasable in Marseilles was an advertisement for Martini vermouth. With Helen as first assistant, Martha began to consult with French authorities.

In France all danger of bombing had passed, but during the coming winter there was almost certain to be a food shortage which would threaten French children with malnutrition. This was clearly evident to relief workers, but not so clear to local folk, as yet unaware of the drastic changes caused by the debacle. Consequently although the Unitarians had block affidavits, at first there were only a few French applications for American hospitality. By September, however, with the rationing system tightening month by month and all available supplies being drained off to the north, attitudes changed, and the project appeared to be swiftly realizable. The small Unitarian office buzzed with activity. Cables hurtled back and forth across the Atlantic, bombarding Lisbon, New York or Boston, and they replying. Often it took days for cables to reach their destination in either direction, and this inevitably led to misunderstanding and more cables. At about the time a set of application blanks was distributed the regulations somewhere might be changed, and the contracts would have to be altered. Every day some government—French, American, Spanish or Portuguese—would change a ruling. What with affidavits, guarantees, guarantors material and moral, fathers in the occupied zone, divorce papers left in Paris, complications of nationality—child traveling with or without parents—with all this, sending a child to America was no simple business. But eventually a list of fifty French children's names was ready to be presented to the prefecture in Marseilles.

Alas, the day before we were about to submit this list, Vichy issued a new order: all exit permits would be issued in Vichy itself, not in Marseilles. It took three weeks of lobbying in that already wintry watering place to convince one official after another that the odd American offer should be accepted. Most of the Vichy officials had never heard of American hospitality to British children. After a toilsome ascent of the bureaucratic ladder, the project reached the desk of the Minister of Foreign Affairs himself—and he turned it down. The French government found the proposal unacceptable. French families must not be separated. French children might be brought into contact with ideas not in line with those of the government. And, anyway, French children were in no need of help. Reluctantly the government agreed that, as an exception, a French child with relatives in the States might go there for a visit.

But there were hundreds of other children whose parents had begged for them to be included on the Unitarian list. Many of the refugee parents, already marked by the German commissions and hence unable to leave France legally, hoped at least to move their children into the free world. American homes and hearts were open, transportation was available: why not take these more needy youngsters instead? The Committees in the United States cabled agreement, and a new rat race began.

Winter was near, no one knew how long the present favorable situation might last: haste was necessary. The fact that many of these refugee children already had American visas simplified matters to some extent, but the complications encountered in arranging to bring this small group into safety were almost unbelievable. Three Czech children, Aryan, had a father in the British army. This was hard for Vichy to swallow, but the youngsters got their passes. One family of six had relatives in the States, but one child had been born in the Cameroons and she had to have a separate U.S. quota number. Another, born in America, had to have her own passport, since both French exit permits and Spanish transit visas for Americans differed from the rest. The father of one boy was a political prisoner in Spain, and the mother made two clandestine trips across the border to secure necessary signatures. One cultured Austrian family, facing literal starvation because of forced unemployment, decided to send their two daughters with the Unitarian group, although they never expected to see them again. Another couple, with one experience in a camp behind them and another inevitable as soon as their slender means were exhausted, brought their ten-year-old boy to us. At least he would be spared the degradation of another term in camp.

Finally twenty-five children had their vaccination certificates, their identification bracelets, their U.S. and French and Spanish and Portuguese travel documents. All twenty-five with their parents were assembled in Marseilles, ready to leave. Then the Portuguese changed their minds and announced that the names for the entire group must be forwarded to Lisbon for individual visas, issued from there. The suspense was terrific. Each day parents would come to the office, asking if the departure date had been fixed. There were recurring rumors that southern France would be occupied by the Germans within a week. One mother, on the eve of the actual departure, disappeared with her two boys who were scheduled as members of the group. Months later the police told us they had traced her departure in a plane apparently bound for Britain, where her husband was an officer in the RAF. At last the little caravan got away, by rail to Lisbon and thence by ship. A small book could be written about what became of these young immigrants in their new country.

Helen's report to America said: "When the first father came to our office and left his ten-year-old daughter in our hands, suddenly it came to us what America meant to the distracted people of this old world. Here were we, perfect strangers, having put in our charge the dearest thing a mother and father own, just because we represented that country which has always stood for liberty and the rights of the individual; which in the past has shown how big its heart was by sending help to sufferers thousands of miles away; and which now was opening its homes as haven for the coming generation of Europe. As one would-be emigrant said to one of our consuls: 'For you *we* are just numbers, but for us *you* are the god who has the right to open the gates of the promised land or keep shut that door and condemn us to despair.' You would have to be here to understand all that American generosity can mean in times like these."

ten

THE BIGGEST EXPORT
PROJECT

O<small>N</small> MY FIRST VISIT TO MAR-
SEILLES I had been astonished to find a Czechoslovak consulate
in operation. Closed for months after the outbreak of war, it
had been reopened by an energetic and courageous consul
who came down from Paris. "Of course it's illegal," he told
me, "but we have some good friends in Vichy, and we'll keep
this place open as long as possible."

The small waiting room in his office was jammed with
sometimes importunate petitioners. Some were civilians, but
a far larger number were men of the Czechoslovak units of
the French army, still wearing their battle-blue French uniforms. They had been fighting too close to the front at the
time of the debacle to escape via Atlantic ports, as had most
other foreign groups.

I had worked with Czech Aid for a year in Paris, and once I was settled in Marseilles I arranged that this organization would help the consulate. The resultant complete collaboration eventuated in our opening a separate Czechoslovak office registered under the name "American Friends of Czechoslovakia." The staff, recruited mostly from among refugees, handled all relief problems, leaving the consul to exercise such official and unofficial functions as were necessary, for as long as he could. We thought by having two offices it would be possible for one to continue functioning in case the police should close the other. This was just what happened four months later. After the arrest of the consul and the official closure of his office, most of the consulate personnel were added to the list of our employees and so, under the flag of an American organization, much of the normal consular activity could be continued. One difference between the two organizations was that, while the consulate had only scanty funds for material relief, the Czechoslovak Aid continued to have money nearly adequate for all its purposes, including some of the most bizarre operations in southern France, several of them pursued in intimate collaboration with the consulate.

I was surprised at the ease with which the *ad hoc* staff I recruited for our Czech Aid became a team. All young men (the director was thirty-four), their rough experiences of the recent past had given them a maturity of judgment far beyond their years. Chosen from among the demobilized Czech and Slovak soldiers, they served unto the end with a loyalty to their fellow countrymen and a courage that was wholly admirable.

Czech Aid's nonmilitary clientele consisted of some eight hundred civilians, some unemployed or unemployable, members of families that had been living in this area before the war, workers from the Gardanne mines or small tradesmen, some refugees from the north, mostly Jewish, some discarded from the foreign labor battalions that had now begun to enroll all the able-bodied men available. Avoiding relief in the form of cash allowances as far as possible, the Aid helped many people find employment, either in French enterprises or in projects we created ourselves. Other agencies were requested to refer to us all Czechoslovak cases. Anyone with a Czechoslovak passport, regardless of race, religion or politics, was given all possible care. This principle was maintained throughout the war, despite some criticism at the outset because of the abnormally large proportion of Jews among the refugees.

One of our earliest projects was what we called the "export business." There were nearly a thousand battle-worn Czechoslovak soldiers who had to be gotten out of France. Czechoslovakia was now a German protectorate; any Czech who had fought the Nazis was considered a traitor and would be shot the moment he fell into enemy hands.

Thanks to a combination of French patriotism and American funds it was possible to slip an occasional small group of these men over the Pyrenees passes into Spain. Of course the Spanish police arrested them, but influential Czechoslovak friends in Madrid usually succeeded in liberating them from the internment camp at Miranda de Ebro within a month or two. From there they were forwarded to Britain. This trickle of a few men each week was pitifully slow. We couldn't march a thousand men over those mountain paths, and every week the threatened German occupation of southern France came nearer. So, together with the consulate, we went into the export business on a large scale.

Most of the local arrangements were made verbally, and of course no written records were kept. Some reports had to go to America, although it was certain the letters would be censored by the Germans. Incoming mail showed the brown or green brush strokes of various acids, where the censor had proved to himself that the letters carried nothing more than what he could normally read. The code we developed for reports to the States may or may not have deceived the Germans and indeed it mystified our friends in America. At any rate reports got through, and the necessary funds for the "business" were made available.

More than a thousand of the Czech soldiers were held under French surveillance in their former training camp at Agde, a small town on the Mediterranean coast east of Perpignan. Our letters began to report that the "Associated Gas Development Enterprise" was going well: "We have made some small sales already, and expect things to move in a big way next week." YMCA headquarters in New York had not been informed about our helping Czechs to escape, so when I wrote that "our business enterprises continue as I reported. Dealing with perishable goods makes time a factor of the greatest importance, and uncertain conditions involve frequent delays," New York generously replied: "You speak of having a business enterprise of which you have written previously, but I have no recollection of any such letter. It must have been lost en route. At all events, I am glad to know that all goes well, at least for the moment, and that you have made considerable progress. We did receive your cable asking us to send you a thousand dollars via Geneva, but whether that was related to the business enterprise, I don't know. We assumed it was for the regular program."

At that time Marseilles fishing boats, because of their usefulness in bringing food to the city, received almost normal rations of gasoline. Most fishermen, however, were known to think it more profitable to dispose of this gas on the black market than to spend hours of toil on fishing operations. I wondered if we could take advantage of this situation for our own purposes. We learned that for fishing boats there was only a loose harbor control. One of our Czech Aid men developed excellent contacts with the fisherfolk, and then for a time we could put a dozen Czech soldiers on one of these boats every few days, and land them on the Spanish coast.

Vichy's constantly increasing control of everything in southern France, however, made this an increasingly hazardous operation, not only for the skipper but also for his cargo —we could not risk letting Czechs fall into German hands. A letter to the American Friends of Czechoslovakia in New York explained the situation: "As you know, considerable time was devoted to a thorough study of the market, and of conditions governing export, especially in the constantly changing situation resulting from the armistice. Furthermore, we have been forced to give more than usual attention to the warehousing and care of our special type of goods awaiting export. We discovered that many bales had to be rewrapped, due to weather conditions encountered on their arrival here. This has involved considerable expense, but we believe the final profit will be enhanced, rather than diminished, due to the maintenance of the goods in first-rate condition.

"The actual shipping operation itself has been complicated by the difficult conditions on the Mediterranean or by rail, via Spain. From your own experience you will realize the difficulties involved in transportation across Spain and Portugal.

"Despite this, we have already dispatched half of our entire stock, and other bales are moving. In view of the short season let us assure you that we are bending every effort to clear our warehouse before it is too late. At present we have confidence of being able to do this."

At first we hoped this export by fishing craft and the passage of small groups of men over the mountains at the Port Bou end of the Pyrenees would continue long enough to put most of our soldiers back into service in Britain. We needed only three months.

Then came the chance for an export deal on a scale commensurate with the number of Czech veterans and the danger they faced. One of our Czech Aid men reported that in the harbor at Marseilles there was a small Yugoslav ship. She could carry six hundred men, crammed into her hold. Why not have her ferry them across to North Africa? Yugoslavia had not yet experienced Hitler's "spite" bombing of Belgrade and was still a neutral country, but most Yugoslavs were already definitely "neutral against the Nazis." We cautiously approached the captain of the ship. Although the Czech consulate lacked funds for civilian relief, there was no shortage of money for military purposes, so that our proposal to the captain meant an attractive business deal for him, apart from political considerations. After a day or two of bargaining, the captain said yes.

As neutral shipping was subject only to ordinary French controls in port, we should be able to move our anti-Nazi cargo without much difficulty—if—There were several large ifs. They were overcome one after another, largely because many Frenchmen felt, after Munich, like a Paris professor who told me, "For the first time in my life, I am ashamed of being French." This tender conscience regarding things Czechoslovak explained many concessions accorded us by the Pétain government, or rather by some officials of that government, throughout the war.

Harbor inspectors in Marseilles readily agreed to permit the Yugoslav ship to leave without too close inspection, if they could be protected by an authorization—verbal of course, not written—from Vichy. Our first visit to the capital in this connection was encouraging. The two ministries we interviewed, National Defense and Foreign Affairs, agreed in principle, but warned us we must work fast. Back in Marseilles, plans were perfected for the ship to put in at a tiny, neglected harbor near Agde, and the final diplomatic assault of Vichy began.

We already knew who were our friends in Vichy, and we had their confidence to such an extent that I could serve as messenger between them when they could not risk being seen in consultation. I could even venture to argue for acceptance of our proposal.

Vichy bureaucracy was still in a state of confusion, but it had carried over from better times the diplomatic habit of buck-passing. Soon we found that we had to deal with six departments, instead of only Foreign Affairs and Defense:

Merchant Marine was involved, and Commerce and two others. All six finally agreed to put the whole question of moving the Czechoslovak veterans up to the highest authority. If "Foreign Affairs," probably with the consent of Marshal Pétain, accepted the project, the other ministries would fall in line.

Calls on various men of influence during the next few days kept them and us in suspense. Any day now German control of all shipping might be extended to the Mediterranean. One man could report that the Ministry of Transport "had no objection." Another would say that one man we had approached was afraid to take any risk, and would suggest a third who was even supposed to be a de Gaullist. We had one bad fright when a messenger I sent to a Monsieur Roget in the Foreign Office achieved an audience with another gentleman of the same name. The wrong Monsieur Roget must have been puzzled by the message, but, so far as we knew, never interfered with our plans. The five-day wait necessary before a decision could be arrived at during the next weekly interministerial conference seemed endless.

I made a hasty trip to Marseilles to be sure everything there was in readiness. It was, but when I spoke of waiting five more days the director groaned. "Half the people in the harbor already know about our Yugoslav ship. In five days Berlin could have the story." Everyone was sitting on the edge of his chair: six hundred men in Agde were kept on the alert, to be able to move to the ship on a half hour's notice. On my return to Vichy the Minister of Defense assured me our plan would be approved. Foreign Affairs said it was supporting the project, but no one could predict Pétain's attitude. The long wait ended late one evening: the decision was favorable. I left by a 4:00 A.M. plane to take the good news to Marseilles.

What happened in the few hours between that word given at Vichy and the next morning will never be known. Did the Germans get wind of the Czechoslovak export plan or was it a simple coincidence that by the time the Marseilles authorities

could be seen that same morning a new order had come
through forbidding any ship to leave any Mediterranean port
without a check by both German and Italian officials, in
addition to the French? In any case, the "biggest export
project" was dead.

Another scheme, to have a dozen fishing craft, each with
twenty stowaways, meet a British destroyer a few miles out
in the Mediterranean, never got beyond the preliminary
planning stage. By the end of August even the small leakage
of Czechoslovak soldiers over the border into Spain, or around
the end of it via a few fishing boats, had almost stopped. Other
methods of keeping approximately five hundred Czechs out
of Nazi hands had to be devised.

Once the comparatively large-scale, extralegal emigration
carried out during the first few months after the debacle
became impractical, we announced the policy of "operating
within the framework of existing law and in closest collaboration with all French authorities." This useful collaboration
continued until the end of the war.

eleven

CZECHS
HELP THEMSELVES

O UR WEEKLY CZECH AID STAFF
meetings were always interesting. Sometimes we would be
discussing a typical case, requiring a decision in principle;
sometimes it was a matter altogether individual. "Here is a
letter that came to my YMCA office marked 'personal,' " I
might report. "This Frantisek Hampl puts up a very good case
for himself." "Oh, Hampl," one of the young veterans would
reply, "everybody knows him—he was the worst drunkard
in our company."

Once the existence of the "Centre d'Aide" became known,
appeals for help flowed in from all corners of southern France.
The following letter, in better English than most, was typical
of thousands we received:

"Permit me to explain my sad case to you. My husband is

sixty years old, of Czechoslovak nationality and non-Aryan.
I am of Dutch origin, but a Czechoslovak by marriage. We
have a daughter of 12 years. We were living in Brussels, until
May 1, 1940. At the time of the German invasion, my husband,
my daughter and I fled from Belgium, and we are now in
distress. All our money and our investments are in England,
we cannot get a cent because the banks have told us that all
fortunes were blocked. The reserves we have taken with us
are exhausted and it is impossible for my mother to send us
money from Brussels or from Holland. We are obliged to
live on the allocation which France is willing to give us, i.e.,
26 francs a day for three persons.

"Now it is forbidden to us to be repatriated as it is forbidden
to the British, Polish, Jews and Czechoslovaks. On the other
hand we are considered as Belgian refugees because we came
from Brussels and there is a danger that the allocation of the
city of Clermont-Ferrand ceases at the 15th of September.
Besides, winter is coming and we have nothing for the cold
and the rain, neither clothes nor shoes, neither for the child
nor for my husband who is very weak and suffers from a
nervous shock. This is the reason why I write the letter in his
place. Besides, Czechoslovak citizens have no right to medical
help nor medicine, as I was told at the city hall. You will
understand what that means in my case. I enclose herewith
the certificate from my doctor in Brussels.

"In view of the fact that we cannot go back to Brussels,
that we have no means of existence nor clothes for the winter
and that it is quite probable that the allocation will be stopped
soon, I ask you with all my heart, and especially because of
my little girl, to help us in our desperate situation."

Sometimes there was a hint of criticism along with the
appeal: "The undersigned, refugees from Belgium, of Czechoslovak nationality, resident in Montauban, respectfully request some sort of aid for the writers. We are here in the
clothes we came in, one suit, one pair of shoes, and these we
have had to use all the summer, so it is literally falling off us.

For the 10 francs refugee allowance we receive from the French government, you cannot buy anything, in view of the high cost of living here, and we are not permitted to seek employment, so we address our request to you. Further we ask your advice, what is to become of us, or when and how? It is very surprising to us that here in Toulouse the Poles have an office, but there is no hint of anything for Czechs." Signatures certified by the Mayor of Montauban.

While each case was special, with nearly a thousand men on our list we in Czech Aid had to plan for groups and group action. Our first long-term project of this sort was the Château de la Blancherie, on the outskirts of Marseilles. A rambling old edifice which once had been painted pink, it was set in thirty acres of ground, with ancient plane trees outlining what once were graveled walks. Like Claracq, it had been unoccupied for years. La Blancherie would afford lodging for one hundred fifty men, and after extensive repairs the place was much more inviting than the cheap hotels of Marseilles, the only possible other lodging for penniless Czechs. At first it was necessary to persuade men to enter the château and agree to the discipline, however limited, that was needed to maintain order in so large a group still suffering from nerve-racking war experiences. Opinion veered quickly, however, and soon there was a long waiting list.

Once the house was in order, the men turned to clearing space for extensive gardening. They even had pink-geranium beds and graveled paths beneath the umbrella pines. Rabbits and hens were purchased, and once the gardens began to produce, this working colony was actually self-supporting. The men began to raise pigs on a large scale, using kitchen refuse from city restaurants as feed. In the early-morning hours of any day, the colony's little donkey cart would be seen "collecting" at the back doors of the best eating places in town. The garbage was then cooked in two enormous army field kitchens someone had discovered. The pork production was so successful that by the end of 1940 the Château was shipping sausages to Czechoslovaks still living on a near-starvation diet in the camps.

In addition to being a successful business enterprise, the colony served several nonmaterial purposes. First, it was a sorting center. Men came to the Château out of nowhere—escaped war prisoners, men invalided out of the foreign labor battalions in the mines, ex-soldiers who for one reason or another had left the military camp at Agde. Our aim in the Czech Aid was to locate as many as possible of these men in jobs they were fitted to handle. After a man had spent a few weeks in the Château, it was apparent what sort of worker he was, how he adjusted to life in a social group, what his capacities, as well as his weak points, were. With this data in hand, a man could be confidently recommended to a French employer or sent out to one of the Czech farms we were setting up.

The Château served also as a rehabilitation institute. Here was Alois Havlicek, who had suffered terrible experiences in Nazi prisons and then the merciless regime of the foreign labor gangs. At the Château he was completely asocial, rarely spoke to anyone, sometimes even failed to observe house rules. The colony director found out that at home Alois had been the village shoemaker. Our hundred fifty men needed a lot of shoe repairs, so the necessary equipment was found, a real cobbler's bench, with hammers and awls and nails, and Alois was installed in a small room where he could work at his trade. The change in the man was almost miraculous: within a few weeks he was a happy, cooperative member of this large family.

Then there was Frantisek Kafka, peasant and ex-soldier, who came to La Blancherie a confirmed drunkard. The wise director gave him the job of caring for Artie, the lop-eared donkey that hauled the cart collecting kitchen refuse and did the transportation errands for the colony. A responsible farm job in the company of sober, industrious men worked the change desired in Frantisek. He and Artie became inseparable companions. Never was a donkey given such cosmetic care. When they were not on the road, Frantisek could usually be found in the stable, talking to Artie as he combed the donkey's gray mane or oiled his shiny hoofs.

Another special operation at La Blancherie was the dental service. It took considerable diplomacy before the French military authorities would release the dental equipment the Czechoslovak Aid had established in Agde, but eventually it was moved to the Château, and a capable team of ex-soldier dentists installed. Before long the team was serving not only residents and the procession of our men passing through Marseilles, but was operating for Czechoslovak children in the city a dental service unknown in the public schools.

A further result of the work of the Château was even more important. Taking a hundred idle men off the city streets helped relieve the police dossiers. Soon the enterprise with its group of well-behaved men busy producing their own food so gained the confidence of the police that the Château became a veritable city of refuge. Once a man was received in La Blancherie, no matter what sort of documents he possessed, or even if he had none, the police accepted our guarantee for him and caused him no trouble. It was usually possible to secure for any resident the necessary travel or residence permits. At a time of such general disorder and scarcity, the fact that a large building and extensive fallow land had been reclaimed greatly impressed French authorities and facilitated our obtaining permission for other Czech Aid projects.

By this time the Germans were so put to it for manpower that a Czech would scarcely be shot as a traitor, but would simply be assigned to building coast defenses for the conquerors. Provided the war did not last too long, he might have a fifty-fifty chance of survival. We had no thought of taking this risk.

If we could not export men out of the Nazis' reach, the only other possibility was to hide them. How are you to hide several hundred able-bodied men? The flourishing gardens of La Blancherie provided a suggestion. In central France many farms, the soil worked out a generation ago, had been abandoned. The Corrèze province, its rural population reduced by half in the past fifty years, and well off the beaten track in the hill country of south-central France, had many such farms. Putting idle men to work producing their own food would be a good thing in itself, and in this out-of-the-way corner of the country they might escape the notice of the Nazi control commissions. Furthermore, none of their production would benefit Germany.

First we rented one farm that could house forty men, and, as the experiment proved successful, six others in the same region were leased. These farms began a new chapter in the history of agriculture in that part of France. Like the La Blancherie property, these farms required basic rehabilitation. The farmstead known as Lapeyre was typical. The huge moss-grown stone house with "1813" chiseled in the keystone over the door had been unused for ten years before the Czechoslovaks came there. It was late June 1941 when the first lease was completed, and if anything was to be grown before autumn on a farm at that altitude every hand should have been busied at plowing and planting. But with all their urgent farm work, the men had also to make the house habitable. The cellar was a lake three feet deep. Broken windows needed a hundred panes of glass: cartloads of rubbish had to be carried out of the house.

Visiting Lapeyre in October, I could report: ". . . cleanliness and order everywhere. Electric light and power has been installed. Every room has been calcimined and doors and windows will be painted this week with paint our men have almost miraculously been able to buy in a country where every sort of building material is extremely scarce.

"One side of the great living room is filled by a fireplace large enough to roast a whole sheep, and this room serves as a dining room and kitchen also. The only cooking stove available thus far is too small for cooking for forty men, so meals are prepared in caldrons over the open fire, just as when the house was built. Although the furniture is limited to beds, plus a few homemade benches and chairs, there are framed Uprka drawings on the walls of each room, adding a touch of color. There is a radio, a small but growing library, and musical instruments for those who can play. In part of the half-basement where the tractor will be stored in winter, a turning lathe and other woodworking tools have been installed. Powered by the tractor, these will provide profitable occupation during the winter, and the YMCA has undertaken to purchase for use in the camps all the toys and parlor games (chess, dominoes, etc.) the men of Lapeyre can produce.

"No one who has not lived in the French provinces can imagine how backward and neglected is all agriculture in this part of the country. Peasants are still using the methods and tools of the seventeenth century. They use their scrubby little cows as draft animals; they plow their fields only superficially, and when our men began plowing their fields twice —once for turning over the surface and then later for depth— the neighbors inquired why they made so much work for themselves. Our men have cut hay from meadows untouched for fifteen years. Although they arrived at Lapeyre the very end of June, they incurred the mild ridicule of their neighbors by sowing buckwheat and planting 10,000 cabbages. The neighbors were sure these would never produce before autumn. The day I visited Lapeyre the brown-stemmed buckwheat was being harvested, an excellent crop, and over half the cabbages were already fine, firm heads.

"Our men have established themselves thoroughly in the community, having made a favorable impression by furnishing extra help, free, for their neighbors' threshing or other special work, and have created a real sensation by fulfilling the necessary formalities to secure government subsidies for the owners of two of the farms. No one in the commune had ever heard of subsidies before. Our farms are going to be a genuine educational influence in this community."

The tractor at Lapeyre was one of only six in the whole province. This was a "modern" machine, burning fine-cut blocks of wood instead of the now rare charcoal. The gas-producing apparatus was carried in a small trailer behind the tractor itself. If ever there was a struggle with the soil, it was here. The huge machine roared across the field, making a noise like a battle with howitzers, turning over the rich brown loam, untilled for fifty years. Roots as thick as a man's wrist had to be cut and torn out. The heavy sod and tangled roots would clog the twin plows, requiring frequent halts for cleaning.

The young man who rode over the plows had hands and feet busy in constant and violent acrobatics, breaking up the sods, pulling up the roots to make the stops for cleaning-out as few as possible. Feeling as much responsibility as the driver, he could have replaced him if necessary. He had been a type-setter in Moravia. The driver, a huge man with a torso bare and bronzed by the sun, glasses hiked up on his forehead, would no more think of having anyone else handle his machine than a jockey his favorite race horse. He had once been a taxi driver in Vienna.

By good fortune, among our Czech veterans were two trained agronomists, and thanks to their counsel agricultural success could be achieved that was undreamed of by the local peasantry. Soil analysis showed a deficiency of lime, and by some wangling the Czechs acquired the last available carload to spread over their fields. Local peasants wondered audibly at this "waste of good money." Later, artificial fertilizers being no longer obtainable, our men organized the collection of wood ashes from bakeries in Marseilles and applied these to a large field of rye which had been severely damaged by a late spring frost. The eight tons of wood ashes covered all but one small corner of the field. By harvesttime all but that one corner had produced a magnificent stand of rye, five feet high.

Within the first year our farms began serving other Czech-

oslovaks in unoccupied France. Food parcels went regularly
to Czechoslovaks still in camps and now on near-starvation
rations. Food could be shipped to Marseilles and placed at the
disposal of the prewar Czech colony there. With the first
autumn harvests in, about five hundred Czechoslovaks, including one hundred thirty children at a colony at Vence, were
completely independent of French sources of food. A high
point of success came when two carloads of potatoes from
our farms supplied all the Czechoslovaks in Marseilles with
stocks for the winter, and this from a province where the
local folk had insisted that the land would not produce
potatoes—they never had grown there.

As in La Blancherie, these farms developed nonmaterial
values surpassing the material. They provided education for
the variegated types of men themselves, as well as for the
neighboring peasantry. The two agronomists ran a series of
lectures buttressed by a small library of agricultural texts,
giving theoretical background for the daily tasks. The men
read eagerly the agricultural technical books we put into their
library. Of course our men learned from the local people as
well. In the early days one of the men came to the farm
manager with a puzzled look on his face: "I yoked the cows
for plowing just as usual, but they simply go round in a circle
—what is the matter, do you suppose?" An old woman who
lived in a small house on the place happened to be going by.
"Why," she said, "you have got Daisy on the wrong side of
Bossy. Just change places, and they will be all right."

Another educational product of the farms was accomplish-
ment in teamwork. Taking a hundred-odd men of ages
ranging from the veteran of the Czechoslovak Legion in
World War I in Russia to an ex-student aged eighteen, and
making them into an effective and congenial team was no
small achievement in itself. The man in charge of all these
farms was an attorney who, himself, had never lived on a
farm. Cheerful and patient, as much interested in reclaiming
men as land, he did excellent work at both. He had a double

task of re-education. Training grocers and medical students to become farmers was one thing. The other was to rehabilitate men who for two years or more, in camps or labor groups, had been thoroughly schooled in all sorts of underhand dealing vis-à-vis the administration—every man for himself. These men now had to be trained to collaborate for the common interest.

Re-education involved a constant battle with prejudice against those who were just learning, more or less awkwardly, a new type of work. We had to struggle against attitudes and ideas: the idea that work on these farms might finish in a few weeks; the longing of some men, for example miners from Belgium, to return to their homes, although this would involve working for the Germans; wrong ideas about France, resulting quite naturally from the crying injustices which these men demobilized from an allied army had met in labor gangs and concentration camps.

Then there was racial prejudice, since our groups were made up of Christians and Jews. From the very start we maintained an absolutely consistent attitude toward this problem. The Constitution of the Czechoslovak Republic gave equal rights to all citizens, regardless of their race or religion, and, in spite of quite abnormal conditions, this was done on our farms. It is pleasant to record that throughout this whole complex of farm projects no serious question of racial distinction ever arose among the men. To be sure, they lived under exceptional conditions and their very lives depended upon success in their enterprise.

And the farms' main objective also was achieved: hiding so many men from the Nazis. The whole project of reclaiming fallow land to produce food in times so close to famine brought these men to the favorable attention of the French people, those in authority as well as their neighbors. One of these latter remarked, "These hundred men have been here for a year, and not one of them has had trouble with the police." Local popularity was demonstrated time and again

when one of our Czechs would be called for recruitment in
the foreign labor battalions. On each occasion the mayor
would make the requisite visit to the prefecture, protesting
that this man was essential to agricultural production, and so
save him from mobilization. Thanks to the splendid reputation
the Czech farmers had built for themselves, the French not
only never reported their presence to the dreaded "Todt
Commission" scouring the country in search of manpower,
but after the Germans came in even warned the Czechoslovaks to scatter into the woods when the Nazis were visiting
that part of the province.

Another type of collaboration with the local population
developed as the French underground grew stronger. Most
of the Frenchmen remaining on farms or in villages had no
experience with modern weapons. Nearly all of our Czechs
had come through actual fighting in Spain or France (or
both), so some of the most capable were moved into villages
where they gave regular military training to local men engaged in "underground army" activities. As these instructors
left our farms, space was freed to lodge a few more Czechs
forced to hide in Marseilles or Toulouse, so that in the end
the farms in the Corrèze saved the lives of several hundred
men.

The Czech Aid had its own children's colony. At the outset
of our work in Marseilles we had faced the problem of the
scores of Czechoslovak children in the camps, some with
their parents, some presumed orphans. Following the Quaker
example, we decided to establish a school-colony for Czechoslovak youngsters. On a hilltop in the valley behind Nice,
with the snowy peaks of the Alps closing the view to the
north and far vistas of the Mediterranean to the south, in the
picturesque village of Vence we found a group of buildings,
constructed a few years before, which had been used until the
war by a private school of such liberal tendencies that its
proprietors spent most of the war years in French concentration camps.

Obtaining permission to open an extra school besides that
in the village of Vence itself required long negotiation, but
finally the property was rented by the YMCA, considered a
more permanent organization than the Czech Aid, on condition (a) that the school would be provisioned with food
imported from Portugal, (b) that its staff would abstain from
all political activity, and (c) that children of school age
would attend the regular village school. To provide food for
our school, thus reducing the costly business of importation
from Portugal, and also to accommodate some of the children's parents, we leased a farm a few miles away, with living
quarters for twenty-five people. We felt this would keep the
parents from too close contact with school life and also give
them useful occupation: raising goats, hens and rabbits, and
working the extensive gardens.

As fast as permission could be secured to liberate them from
the camps, the school buildings were filled with Czech children. By midsummer (1941) we had eighty in residence,
twenty-three under six, forty-nine of grade school age, and
eight between fifteen and eighteen. I had seen some of these
youngsters in the camps, undernourished, without decent
shelter or any semblance of family life, and threatened with
serious moral deterioration by the promiscuity and complete
lack of privacy behind the barbed wire. The difference after
a short time at Vence was almost unbelievable; rosy cheeks
and clear eyes were evidence enough of great improvement,
both physical and moral. Records showed that in six months
these children had gained an average of thirteen pounds each
in weight. Incipient spinal curvature due to the life in the
camps was gone; highly nervous, "difficult" youngsters had
become normal. It was no wonder that in a class of ten-year-
olds, when children were naming great men of the present,
along with Masaryk and Pétain and Roosevelt, one child
named "Mr. Krak," a Czech farmer at Lapeyre. "But we are
naming great men," she was told. "That's why I named him,"
said the girl. "He got me out of Gurs."

The eight snug buildings of the "Christian Home for Children" (we adopted this official name to emphasize our difference from the former ultraliberal occupants) formed a small settlement on this hilltop about a mile distant from the nearest town, a hamlet complete with everything needed for excellent care and training of children. The classrooms were decorated in soft colors, the small dormitories kept in excellent order with each child's things stored neatly in a cupboard beside his bed. There was a huge reservoir for irrigating the extensive vegetable gardens. Here, even as late as November, some of the ten-year-olds would swim under the bright sun of the Riviera. The school was approved by the French government and all education was given in French, save for the older children, who had courses to perfect their native Czechoslovak. The kindergarten occupied a separate building, with small play- and schoolroom combined, and was directed by specially trained personnel.

The school was already filled to capacity when about forty more youngsters came to light as we succeeded in extracting the last Czechoslovak children from the various camps. For weeks we struggled with the problem of making room for them. The hotel at La Gaude, halfway between the farm and the school, seemed to be the answer. Here, a modern three-story building with a dozen rooms had served as combined inn and roadhouse at the edge of the village, but had been closed for about a year. There was running water in every room, balconies and a sunny terrace for winter use, and great plane trees to protect children from too much sun in the summer. Here we moved the kindergarten and its personnel, thus releasing about forty places in the school, into which we put other youngsters. Incidentally, the officials of the community told us how happy they were to have their hotel "disinfected" and put to decent use.

To the problem of caring for children, a new one soon was added: assistance to the Czechoslovaks in Nice itself, fourth largest city in France. Some were refugees, others old folks, still others were active, honest people who could not find employment because they were foreigners. We could offer these people the twelve cents per day allowance which was regulation in all our Czechoslovak aid. Or we could try to provide useful and constructive employment. We chose the latter course.

Just under the hill where the school stood was a fertile valley with the little Cagne River at the bottom of it. Most of this valley, a real wilderness interspersed with ruined houses, had been uncultivated for forty years. We took over a large section on a rent-free basis for nine years, and began the not inconsiderable task of rehabilitation. An old irrigation canal was extended for over a mile, thus providing unlimited water to irrigate the terraced hillside. The "reconstruction team" began turning roofless ruins into livable houses where eventually thirty people were lodged, and the rest of the group of unemployed began clearing and planting the land.

This was a hard job. First, the brush and small trees had to be chopped away, the ground burned over, then terrace walls rebuilt and the debris cleared off. Then the ground had to be turned over by hand to a depth of two feet in order to be sure that weeds rooted there for years would not reappear on the new surface. The soil was what the Russians would describe as "rich enough to spread on bread." Several acres were planted in onions and cabbage, to be harvested in early spring, when potatoes would be planted, these to be succeeded in autumn by a third crop of vegetables. In this mild climate, the land yields three times a year.

Of late there had been much talk in France about reclaiming its thousands of acres of deserted farms. Government funds were available, and by using these our men were able to receive pay for all the work they were doing and for the reconstruction of a dozen small houses as well. The enterprise won general approval in the district, and the Czechoslovak reputation was high. This particular province was so badly in need of food that foreigners were constantly being expelled, and even Frenchmen needed special travel permits to visit it. No better proof of the standing of our enterprise could be offered than the fact that, in spite of the conditions just indicated, permission was given us to import twenty-five adult Czecho-slovaks from the camps, in order to extend our land-reclamation project.

With Czech frugality our men made use of everything. Every tiny corner of land at the school, save the playground, was planted with garden stuff. The remains of a wire fence found on the farm was used to rebuild some dismantled beds. The previous summer, a forest fire near the school had devastated a considerable area. and our men offered to clear this, taking in payment half the firewood obtained. As a result, the whole colony was provided with fuel for a year ahead, this in a country where the finest hotel in Nice could not afford hot water.

In addition to serving the Czechs in Nice, Vence set up a summer camp where, for the two "peaceful" summers granted us, more than a hundred children from the Gardanne coal mines spent their vacations, with good food and a chance to recuperate in the sunshine of the Riviera.

twelve

CHILDREN
BEHIND BARBED WIRE

DESPITE THE SLOWLY INCREAS-
ing number of children's "colonies," like the one at Vence and
the RSCM's Claracq, there were over two thousand children
still in the camps. These presented a special problem, and made
an appeal to which everyone responded.

Relief agencies exerted every effort to improve the situation.
While a few agencies of the Nîmes Committee were specialists
in child care, numerous others were also helping children in
addition to their general programs. French authorities were
usually sympathetic to any suggestion for aid to children. The
French, with their declining population, appreciated more
than anyone else the need to preserve child lives. And the
refugees themselves expressed unselfish concern. As one refugee remarked: "The war has ruined us, but you can still save

the children."

First of all, the youngsters needed food, something better than that served to the adult camp population; rations were steadily decreasing in both quantity and quality as supplies in southern France became exhausted. Switzerland, itself existing on belt-tightening rations, generously allowed the Swiss Aid to Children to export foodstuffs. Other agencies managed to bring stocks from Portugal or even from the United States, as was the case with the American Red Cross. All such supplies had to be distributed with the greatest caution, lest word get about that foreigners in camps were being better fed than Frenchmen themselves.

Securing food supplies was only one aspect of the problem. How are you to operate a children's canteen in a camp when there is no soap for dishwashing? And what about children who cannot come for the daily ration because they have no shoes, or because they are standing in some other ration queue in place of their mother? In the winter, some canteens had to close for lack of fuel.

The children needed clothing and medical attention almost as urgently as food. Here the non-French organizations could provide: they could import from Portugal both clothing and medicines. From the shiploads of supplies the American Red Cross brought into France, a small portion was assigned to the agencies at work in camps. Medical service was assured by a group of physicians who were refugees themselves but still at liberty, and thus able to place themselves at the disposal of the Nîmes Committee agencies. Often these refugee physicians had been of the highest rank in their homelands.

The main effort of the Swiss Aid was directed toward helping the children in camps. Swiss feeding stations were models of neatness and cleanliness. Inside, there was the Swiss flag, posters of Swiss mountain scenery, and the Swiss lady herself, with spotless uniform and welcoming smile. The moral effect of such neatness in the midst of dirt and evil smells was inestimable. Another service for children was brought about by Swiss initiative. Several relief agencies had cooperated to set up a school system where all children were busied during the day, but in the evening children were somewhat in the way in crowded barracks. The Swiss organized a series of children's huts, cheerful with white curtains, pictures, neat cases of games and toys and most important, a stove. Thus a place was provided for children in the evenings. The nurse in charge in one camp said it was a pleasant change to have children coming to her for something other than food. She reported proudly that in one evening she had given out two hundred books from her special children's library.

The schooling of small children was the responsibility of the Unitarian Service Committee. Their kindergartens, with low pine tables and small benches where scores of tots under six played games or drew pictures, were a delight. To anyone who had seen the children a few months earlier, completely wild in the dusty camps, the educational and moral value of the Unitarians' work was apparent. The Unitarians also equipped and often staffed dispensaries and clinics in camps, as well as in Marseilles.

By mid-1941 the Nîmes Committee could register substantial results of its efforts. Under pressure from us, the government liquidated two of the worst camps, Agde and Argelès, at the same time accepting our advice as to where inmates of these two camps should be sent. At one of our Committee meetings, when we were discussing the special problems of children and adolescents in the camps, the Quaker delegate from Perpignan told us of a large permanent army camp, at present unoccupied, near that city. A subcommittee was designated to look into the matter, and at the next month's meeting we had a report and a recommendation. If all mothers and children could be concentrated in this camp, at Rivesaltes, some of our youth problems would be easier to solve. I was asked to see what could be done about this in Vichy. Vichy gave its consent after we had completed some complicated negotiations with the police department and the army about

A shipment of Jews arrives at an internment camp in
Southern France. May, 1941.

JDC photos

A Joint Distribution Committee feeding station. The first
hot meal in days brings smiles to young refugee faces.

Any dwelling became a refuge.

Children separated from their parents are frightened
even of the photographer.

In a camp, all that a family owned might be hung on a nail on the wall.

Old coat finds new owner. This girl, just rescued from an internment camp, wears the first warm clothing available.

JDC photo

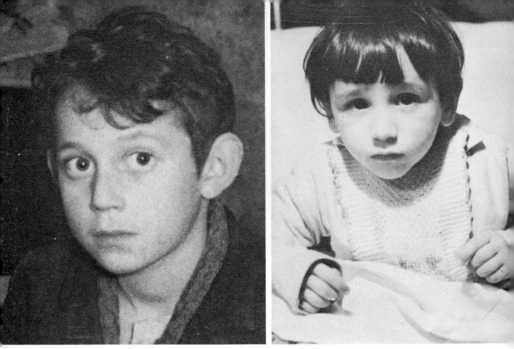

JDC photo

For thousands of children the future was uncertain.

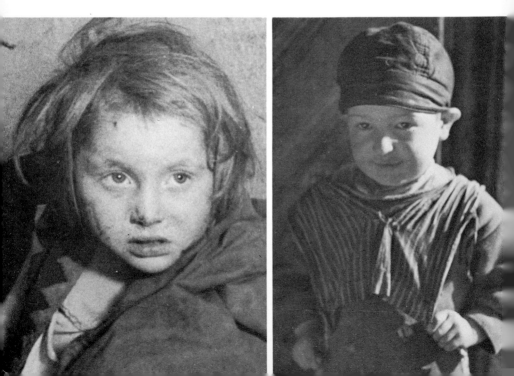

Youngsters from a children's home in Marseilles enjoy
an afternoon at the beach.

Orphans, real or presumptive. Jewish children in a
"colony" in unoccupied France.

JDC photo

These children were removed from camps in time to emigrate to America. They await their sailing, in a child-care center in Marseilles.

JDC photos

Children in a nursery in Limoges. Most of the clothing came from the United States via the JDC.

Entrance to the "foyer" at Rivesaltes. Inside the camps, the YMCA and the French CIMADE worked together. "Just the sight of you . . . is assurance that the world outside still cares."

Men between the ages of eighteen and sixty-five were recruited for the German labor battalions.

Inmates of Rivesaltes cooking "greens." As in all the camps, the food shortage was acute.

People waiting to be loaded into deportation trains at Rivesaltes. Hoping to save their children, parents often made the bitter decision to leave them behind.

the use of military property. In Marseilles the Rockefeller Foundation representative had agreed to serve on a committee to plan the installation and use of the camp, and together with French authorities we all set to work.

Rivesaltes was a barrack-city originally designed to house 50,000 colonial troops; decent brick buildings were set on an arid plain not far from Perpignan. "Arid" was the word: not a tree or a bush could be seen—just a vast expanse of gravel from which the sand had already blown away. When the tramontane, the fierce, cold wind off the Pyrenees, came up it would lift even large pebbles and drive them like bullets across the open spaces. We learned later that the reason this camp had seldom been occupied was because of the serious shortage of water, a lack which was particularly unpleasant during the long Mediterranean summer.

Into the small city of Rivesaltes families were now moved from other camps, together with hundreds of children left orphans after their parents had been deported from occupied France. There were some men in the camp, but its population consisted mainly of women and children. The lodging was passable, although here, as everywhere, there was crowding, poor ventilation and not enough light. Two crude plank shelves, one above the other, served as beds. The top shelf was five feet from the ground, the lower a foot above the floor. Clothing was hung on whatever projection might serve the purpose, and the only storage space for food or other reserves available for the residents on the upper tier was space on a transverse roof beam, if one happened to be near enough. The pitiful row of old cans of all descriptions lining these beams spoke clearly of the inmates' poverty. It was a good thing that extra buildings were available for any cultural purpose desired (management refused to "thin out" the residential barracks) and on the whole Rivesaltes turned out to be the best of our camps.

As elsewhere, the feeding problem in Rivesaltes was acute. All over the camp women built small fires in clusters of stones and cooked for themselves, mostly greens. We saw two boys grubbing among the pebbles for weed roots, and they told us these would be cooked and eaten.

I sometimes watched the distribution of American Red Cross milk to children aged six to fourteen. There were no dishes at Rivesaltes, so each child had to bring his own drinking utensil and a more varied collection of old tin had never been seen. Some children carried tin cans with the top gone, others had old saucepans, and some had what were evidently the bottom of tin drums about eight inches in diameter, cut down to leave a three-inch-deep basin. The less said about the cleanliness of these utensils the better.

The children looked as though they could hold two quarts of milk instead of the pint given them; a boy who said he was twelve looked like a nine-year-old. A girl of ten might easily have been seven. These were Spanish children, now in their third year in internment camps. Some had been born there, and others had fled from Spain with their parents. Some had been orphaned when typhoid swept the camp at Argelès, the children miraculously escaping infection when crowded conditions made impossible any isolation of the sick, and disinfectants were almost totally lacking. The Jewish children, interned less than a year before, were in notably better condition. Each child had to drink all the milk served him and show his dish upside down as he passed the nurse stationed at the exit.

Rivesaltes was the site of the most extensive coordinated project we undertook during those years. Conferences between camp management, the French education authorities, and representatives of our different Nîmes organizations resulted in a school project that included almost all the two thousand children in the camp. It was a typical Nîmes Committee cooperative undertaking. The French government provided teachers and textbooks for the basic school program. The Unitarian Service Committee gave equipment for kindergartens, took care of directed play and courses in handicrafts.

In addition, volunteer teachers gave lessons in a half dozen languages. The Polish YMCA installed one large social center, and the World's Committee YMCA two more. Generous supplementary medical service was assured by a joint committee of Jewish organizations and the Unitarians. With most of the children and their mothers gathered here, Rivesaltes, until the deportations began, was a constructive educational operation.

Rivesaltes was the best we could do for the children if they had to live in a camp. A far better arrangement was to place them in homes or "colonies" outside. The Quakers or the OSE (Jewish Children's Relief Organization) would equip some vacant château or other fairly adaptable property and ask Vichy's permission to move twenty, forty or a hundred children into it. In most cases the French authorities continued the per diem allowance children had received in camps, and by some supplement of this amount on the part of the agency youngsters could be far better cared for than under the official regime of a camp. After a tour of the camps I always had special pleasure in visiting one or another of the colonies. For one thing, children seemed to become more individual in the intimacy of a "family," even if that family was as large as a hundred persons.

For instance, there was dark-haired Yetta, scarred with more terror during her eight years of life than most adults would ever know. Her parents killed in the Warsaw ghetto, she had lived for days in the cellar of a ruined house, without water or light. Some agency had transported her from Poland to find shelter with an aunt in Béziers. Then it was discovered that the aunt, poverty-stricken herself, had no place for Yetta in her one miserable room. Someone else must take responsibility for the child. Yetta found shelter in one of the children's colonies set up by the American Friends Service Committee. This colony was lodged in an old château set on a chestnut-bordered terrace overlooking a broad valley, and it was about as different as could be imagined from the camps most of its wards had left. Much thought and a little paint had made the dusty interior homelike. Each of the dormitory rooms was decorated in a different color, and there were even small framed pictures on the walls.

A Christmas party I attended in this place was something to be remembered. Thanks to American connections, each child had received from some child in the States what was universally called an "American bag," containing riches almost unimaginable: underwear and socks, a sweater, a doll or a mouth organ or a box of paints. In honor of us visitors the youngsters put on a play, *Little Red Riding Hood*, with acting that left nothing to be desired in the way of drama. The woodcutter was a seven-year-old Spanish boy, proud of his blacked-on mustache and sideburns. Yetta was the leading lady who trembled properly before the wolf and kissed the woodcutter as applause began at the close of the play. It was good to see the children smiling and dancing there on the sunny terrace. In this château a few of them could lead something like a normal life, and learn to forget the catastrophes that had cost them their homes and families.

thirteen

SERVICE
IN THE CAMPS

B<small>Y THE BEGINNING OF 1941 THE</small>
outside world began to hear about the camps we were serving.
The New York *Times* carried a two-column article, "Misery
and Death in French Camps." Gurs was the camp most talked
about, but it was by no means unique. Despite the removal of
able-bodied men to work battalions and the trickle of successful emigration, the population of the camps remained stable.
As refugees living outside became indigent, they were forced
to move into the shelter centers. By the end of the year only
a few hundred men and women had been liberated from the
repression camps; the camps for the aged and the invalids were
always filled to capacity.

Food conditions were deplorable: a Friends Service Committee report noted that "what was supplied by the govern-

ment was sufficient for only two thirds of the inmates" of
Gurs. The OSE managed early in the year to take a hundred
children from Gurs to a home they established in Limoges.
From that place came this letter: "I have seen hundreds of
children in Russia, Hungary and Poland after pogroms or
famine, but none like those we have just received from Gurs.
. . . Passengers in the train that brought them were moved
to tears by the sight of the starved youngsters. At Toulouse,
doctors forbade us to move them further, as the children
were too weak to stand more travel."

Each camp had a series of hospital barracks for treating
those in danger of death from undernourishment. Many of
the patients were stricken with famine dropsy: others were
skin and bone—literally.

With camp populations including so many old folks, so
many already ill, conditions were reflected in the mortality
rate; an average of twenty persons per day, at the worst. The
aunt of an American consul at Bordeaux died in Gurs two
weeks after the consul had offered all necessary guarantees
for her release from camp. The camp cemetery told the story:
rows on rows of fresh graves, almost like the day after a
battle, each with a simple marker giving name and date of
death. It was impossible to visit this place without feeling
deep emotion: this promiscuous mingling of Jew and Christian after all the misery that had shadowed the end of their
days was a symbol of the terrible times in which we lived.

Into this "unbreathable atmosphere of human helplessness"
came our various relief agencies. And at once, if only slowly,
improvement began. After blankets and disinfectants, the
most important relief was food. As with all other phases of
relief, feeding in camps was well coordinated: the Joint
Distribution Committee placed in the hands of camp directors
funds for supplementing the adults' ration. By operating in
local markets, agents from camps could purchase foods Vichy
could not even requisition. The Quakers and the Swiss Aid
set up special feeding kitchens. Thanks to the collaboration

of relief agencies, an extra meal given daily was saving literally thousands of lives. For one camp the Swiss Aid gave a daily ration to two hundred men chosen by the camp doctor as the worst cases of malnutrition. The sight of these men was heartbreaking. One day when I visited the camp the day's portion was a plate of hot compote of dried fruits and ten almonds per man. You never saw dishes cleaner than when these men had finished. The girl in charge told me of her campaign to have men shave and wash before coming to be fed, and of the noticeable moral effect on men almost too far gone in misery to care whether they were clean or not.

One of the outstanding instances of cooperation in camps between two agencies was that of the YMCA and the CIMADE, a union of French Protestant youth organizations for refugee service. This group began service to the thousands of French refugees from the northeast at the outbreak of the war. They continued service to their fellow citizens as well as to the largely foreign population of the camps right through to the liberation. Inside the camps, the two organizations planned most of their work together: in foyers supplied and supported by the YMCA, CIMADE provided the staff.

CIMADE and Swiss Aid personnel lived in the camps, but even regular visitation by representatives of other agencies served a positive purpose. One professor in Gurs remarked to me: "Just the sight of you walking through our camp means more than you can imagine. It is assurance that the world outside still cares, and that we are not completely forgotten."

Probably equal in importance with the material aid so generously poured into the camps by some of our relief agencies was the nonmaterial help furnished by others—the religious groups, the European Student Relief, and the YMCA. Within a few months after our services began, libraries had been started in every camp. Thanks to purchases by the YMCA, these quickly grew to significant proportions. The Gurs library, for instance, eventually had over 4,000 books, with a monthly turnover of 10,000, and in some of the ilots the books were read eight times per month. Of the two hundred fifty half-starved men who were given a daily extra feeding by the Swiss Aid, fully half of them would bring library books when they came for their ration, holding the books in their laps or laying them on the table as they solemnly consumed their food.

Books also provided the basis for the hundreds of educational classes and study groups in every camp. Languages were most popular among the courses. Most of the would-be emigrants studied English, but classes ranged all the way from chemistry to Arabic and Hebrew. With so many intellectuals interned, instructors in scores of subjects were available; the lectures benefited both listeners and the speaker, since the latter's preparative work provided time-filling activity. In addition there were trade schools where lawyers or clerks learned to be carpenters or typewriter repairmen or tailors.

We also provided games for the camps, especially chess, checkers and dominoes. Since these items had formerly come from northern France, they were hard to find in local shops, but a group of Czechs in one of the camps set up a workshop in a tumbledown shed and produced the equipment needed. Since we merely took these games and distributed them to other camps, this manufacturing enterprise did not infringe upon the severe regulations prohibiting anyone in a camp from competition with French industry, while it provided some income for men otherwise unable to earn a sou.

Chess sets were made from soupbones gathered from the camp kitchen. Before the bones were used for anything else they were boiled and every bit of grease carefully skimmed off, to be used in the soup these men cooked for themselves to supplement the camp ration. Then the perfectly dry bones were fashioned into chessmen. The prisoners found a way to use lampblack, or something like it, to blacken half the figurines. The chess boards were of highly polished pine with the same black rubbed into alternate squares. A complete hand-made chess set cost us the equivalent of fifty cents, and brought hundreds of dollars' worth of pleasure to men who might otherwise have been sitting idly on their straw sacks.

Then there was music. It usually began with gramophones and records. There was always some prisoner eager to take charge of the YMCA equipment, and camp authorities quickly perceived the value of at least this much music. In Vernet, for instance, one of the "suspect" prisoners, himself a composer, was permitted to visit one section after another (otherwise all communication between sections was forbidden) with concerts of recorded music and to give a talk about the composers and the works on the program.

One day this man was telling me about his activities: "You thought it odd, the last time you were here, when I suggested providing a canary for each barrack. I realized the truth of your objections, but there was need for something to take men out of themselves and help bring them together. If I had thought of a gramophone, I should never have asked for canaries. You have no idea what a record concert does. In several barracks it has become a unique social occasion. Those who have tea put it together and invite all the other inmates, and sometimes the atmosphere is so different from the ordinary that it is almost religious."

These concerts were especially appreciated during the three-hour period of darkness in the barracks between nightfall and the time when lights were turned on. All of France had to economize on electric power, and the camps were no exception.

In a letter home I wrote: "We are now working out a system of exchanging records (those that have not been worn thin already) among the camps. Orchestra music is hard to find in shops, but piano arrangements do almost as well, for in almost every camp there are a dozen musicians who can re-transcribe for orchestra a given overture or symphony. As yet there have been practically no choirs or other singing groups, but really there is little in the life of these camps to inspire song. Perhaps that will come later."

There were many musicians among internees and hence live concerts could be given in almost any camp if only instruments were available. One day two of us went from Marseilles by train to a camp near Toulouse carrying a couple of violins, a cello, a guitar and, in a huge suitcase, a lot of other smaller instruments. We looked like a traveling orchestra and every one of the four times we changed trains, people on the station platform seemed to expect us to break loose with a concert and pass the hat. But when we reached the camp there was no uncertainty about our mission. I happened to know that a young man in this camp had been the director of the opera in a large German city. He was in conference with another American in an adjoining room when we arrived and asked him to come to see us. His face, when he saw the instruments we had brought, was something I shall long remember.

After a concert in Gurs I wrote: "We have come to Section F for the 23rd Sunday-morning piano and violin recital. A hundred people crowd the benches which fill the dingy barrack. The stage is hung with curtains made from army blankets, brown and dirty looking. The violinist is a pupil of Ysaye; the pianist is a young Aryan forced to leave Germany in order to marry a Jewish girl, and now spending his third year in camp. The program consists of sonatas by Mozart and Grieg, and a Schubert Fantasie. This morning's audience is an elite. There are many other concert groups in camp, from the full symphony orchestra to string quartets and jazz. But those gathered for this recital are special lovers of music at its best.

"The music sweeps away every other thought and gray, worn faces are transfigured. A man beside me listens with his head bowed in his hands as though in prayer. For a while everything else is forgotten: the clammy sea of mud surrounding the barrack, the gnawing of chronic undernourishment, even the constant anxiety about possible liberation. For this *is* liberation. And the spirit rises above the things of the flesh, and men find their own pure selves again. As we go out, the librarian, a fine young chap whose wife was lost during an air bombardment somewhere in the debacle of June, 1940, and who still has not lost hope of finding her, shakes my hand in the fellowship of this music and says, 'The week is never the same, if I miss this Sunday-morning concert.' "

In most camps there was a rabbi among the internees. For the other faiths local clergy, often German-speaking, gave most liberally of their time. Their role in raising the morale was supported by a remarkable group of French social workers, mostly from Protestant groups who, to give better service, went to the courageous length of taking residence in the camp, sharing all the discomforts, the lack of heat, the miserable food, with the internees themselves. The fact that someone cared enough to come and live with them gave these workers a unique prestige with the inmates. Their presence also had undoubted influence on the camp management. Here were "free" men and women who knew everything that went on in the camp, who could be very helpful to well-meaning camp directors but a certain hindrance to any crooked dealing by the camp administration. The visits of other representatives of relief agencies served the same purpose. At one time an anonymous letter to the director of Vernet led him to refuse entrance to the only Orthodox priest in the area. It happened that I knew the priest (the YMCA had been covering his travel expenses) and by reassuring the director that the man was not a Communist (!), I was able to secure permission for him to resume his visits.

Eventually most of the camps had a chapel, more or less improvised, or at least a place where religious services could be held. In Gurs each ilot had one barrack set apart for religious, cultural and recreative purposes. High holidays of all faiths were celebrated. Rosh Hashana in 1941 was prepared for weeks in advance, a French Protestant group lending every possible aid. In Gurs on that occasion all ilots were open for two days, with freedom of passage from one to the other, and for the first time wine was legally served in camps. It was a real holiday, long to be remembered.

One day in Marseilles I was introduced to the French Red Cross visitor just in from Gurs. She did not know of my relationship with relief agencies. "Things are getting better all the time," she told me, "thanks to these foreign organizations. We poor French haven't much for ourselves, and of course we're doing all we can for our own refugees, but these organizations, some American, some Swiss, some international, apparently exist just to help refugees."

"What kind of things do they do?" I asked.

"Just about everything to make life more bearable for all those poor people. Those awful barracks had no windows, and it was enough to drive a woman to suicide to sit in the dark all day, every day it rained. Well, someone came with carpenters and installed skylights, and living there became better at once. And now there's a small barrack equipped by a woman's organization from Geneva, for a sewing room."

I knew this was the World's YWCA. She went on: "There are a dozen machines and they are busy from morning till night. Women of all nationalities and ages—you see, that organization provides materials, and even thread, when we French can scarcely find it in our shops. And for these women—lots of them haven't anything but what they wore when they were driven from their homes two years ago—having a chance to make themselves some clothes is wonderful. The lady in charge has found knitting work for mothers so that they can provide a pair of stockings or a bit of extra food for their children—the women will never forget this service.

"And then there are people from some organization (I think some of them are Jewish) who come to talk to those who hope to emigrate to America or the Argentine, or wherever. Sometimes they have money for a refugee, which they leave on deposit at the office for him to use, bit by bit, as camp regulations permit."

The French Red Cross lady was not quite sure whether that

emigration organization was Jewish. At this stage of the war her uncertainty was not surprising. By the end of the war, however, it would have been. One of the dreadful legacies which Hitler bequeathed to Europe and the world was the almost universal consciousness of who is or is not Jewish. Before the Nazis came into power, you might ask the man in the street in France—or even in Germany—if this or that person was a Jew and he would say he had never thought about it. Even many Jews in Germany had scarcely thought of being Jewish until Hitler suddenly set them apart from all "decent citizens."

But after years of anti-Semitic propaganda the poison was lodged deep in the public mind. Peaceable citizens saw their fellow townsmen deprived of all they possessed and carted off to Jewish camps or worse, they learned from the newspapers that Jews were responsible for almost any national disaster, present or past, or that the whole racial group was secretly plotting to take over control of the world, as "proved" by the Protocols of the Elders of Zion, and they came involuntarily to make the immediate distinction—Jewish or not? Generations must pass before this pattern of thought disappears from the public mind.

fourteen

VICHY 1941
"LABOR, FAMILY, FATHERLAND"

THE YEAR 1941 WIT-
nessed steady devolution of the Vichy government toward a
totalitarian state more and more closely allied to Hitler. In
January the French Republic disappeared. This was evidenced
by the changed title of the *Journal Officiel of the French Republic* with "State" inserted instead of "Republic." The almost
sacred motto "Liberté, Fraternité, Egalité" was dropped from
all French coinage and instead the Pétain slogan was used, "Labor, Family, Fatherland"—whatever that was supposed to
mean. More and more German "delegations" and "commissions" added to the crowding in the cities, particularly in the
better hotels: nowhere in Germany or other occupied terri-
tories was living so comfortable.

About this time Vichy closed all French frontiers to prevent

its citizens from leaving to join the Allies, and then came
Pétain's proclamation of himself as supreme and sole authority
in France. The typical effort of a dictatorship to control men's
minds was exemplified in Pétain's order that July 14, Bastille
Day, France's greatest patriotic holiday, should be observed
not with the usual gaiety and fireworks but as a day for medi-
tation on the miseries of France.

With Pétain's appointment of Admiral Darlan to chief military authority, Vichy France became virtually an ally of
Germany. Darlan's ancient anti-British prejudices were well
known, and no one could have been better suited to ally
Pétain with Hitler. In this connection the story went around
Marseilles that the Cardinal of Paris had remarked that in
times like these he would not mind dying—but if he did, he
would like to return to Paris ten days later to see if his seat had
been taken by an admiral.

The steady change in policy was accompanied by corre-
spondingly frequent changes in personnel. One of the most
vexing aspects of dealing with a revolutionary government was
that at about the time arrangements had been completed with
some high authority he would disappear, and one would have
to begin all over again with his successor. In one painful case,
the Coordination Committee had achieved approval of its
camp program from one department and then the whole
authority was transferred to a rival department that seemed
to feel duty bound to resist in principle everything the previous
department had authorized. It took weeks of patient insistence
to modify this attitude, with consequent delay for many of
our projects. And even then one was never sure whether the
high authority who had agreed to the plans would remain in
office long enough to issue the promised orders.

All this confusion in government organization helped con-
firm the authority of the police. Sometimes it seemed that they
represented the only real authority left, and they acted after
the manner natural to police. In Marseilles, in one month, a
series of indiscriminate roundups of all foreigners terrorized

the city. The police invaded cheap hotels at six in the morning
and hauled men off to be imprisoned on a ship in the harbor.
It was said that this measure was to recruit labor for the coming
harvest. Since these hotel raids seemed always to start at six,
one of my friends used to leave his room every morning at
five and spend the day in hiding at the edge of town.

When visiting Vichy I always had to report to the chief of
the National Police. He was an energetic and jumpy person
who was quoted as having said, "Every foreigner is an enemy."
By good luck I had been able to establish quite frank relations
with this man, and he seemed to give credit to most of the
items we presented. On one occasion I reported on the most
recent meeting of the Coordinating Committee and presented
a list of names of organization representatives for whom we
were seeking general permits to visit camps. The police chief's
response was typically bureaucratic: He pulled out a copy of
a letter he had addressed to me and sent "through channels"
via the governor of our province. Although the letter was
dated a month earlier, I had not received it. The police chief
read out one paragraph indicating that as chairman of the
Coordination Committee (in one sentence it was called the
"Lowrie" Committee) I had the right to request our local
governor (préfet) to deliver visitation permits to anyone I
named. It was useful to know that the police had this much
confidence in us.

The second item we discussed was a trade school for one
hundred fifty boys aged fourteen to eighteen, organized by
the Jewish society ORT. This had been presented in principle
before, but now I came with a specific project for a specific
place. The police chief granted permission to take these boys
and their teachers from the camps and put them into a small
château rented by ORT. The French authorities would transfer to the school the per diem allowance for the camps, and of
course would supply the necessary police guard around the
place. We offered to open this school to any boys in the village
who might wish to take advantage of first-class technical in-

struction, but this was not accepted. "It is better that French children should not mix with foreigners," the chief said. What he meant was that Aryan children should not have contact with Jewish people. But, anyway, our project was authorized.

Then I had a question: What were the exact conditions under which a person confined in a camp might be liberated? There were hundreds who could present guarantees of maintenance, but up to now no specific statement of the financial and other conditions required for liberation had been announced. No progress was made at this meeting either, but my conviction was renewed that liberation for Aryans was one thing, and for non-Aryans quite another.

Another project for which we needed Vichy approval was a home for five hundred convalescent invalids who because of lack of space had been pushed out prematurely from the two big camps for the sick. One of our organizations offered to provide such a center and thus give five hundred more people the chance of living outside the camps. This project was accepted in principle, but we would have to come to Vichy again and propose a specific place. In connection with this project I presented a complete list of men in the internment camps, showing age, nationality, religion and—this was the purpose of the list—their professions. The police chief was glad to have this, but was evidently annoyed that the information had to be given him by private organizations rather than his own personnel.

The chief hesitated at my next request. I presented a list of twenty children, the last Czechoslovak youngsters remaining in camps. We wanted to transfer them to our Czechoslovak children's colony at Vence on the Riviera. He read the names over to himself: "Aren't these children Jewish?" "Perhaps, monsieur, but for us they are just Czechoslovaks," I told him, "and they will certainly be happier in Vence than in camp." "All right," the great man said, "I agree," and he told his secretary to prepare the necessary orders for release.

The difference between occupied and nonoccupied France was fast disappearing. While the general public in southern France already saw that France's only hope lay with the Allies, the group around Pétain, after several "purges," had come almost completely to favor collaboration with the Germans. Unoccupied France was almost as thoroughly under Nazi control as if there were formal occupation. The French police now appeared to take orders directly from the Gestapo. Behind every customs official, as one crossed the line into Switzerland, stood a man in civilian clothes who, everyone knew, was a German. The number of commissions or other excuses for introducing Germans into our part of France was increasing. In May I reported: "We hear that a German naval commission is building a reassembly plant at a Mediterranean port, to reconstruct submarines that are to be dismounted and transported across France by canal." When in 1944 we first drove back from Switzerland to a liberated Paris we were puzzled to see in some villages, otherwise undamaged by war, that the corners of houses bordering the route had been bull-dozed away. We learned that these house corners had prevented the passage of German submarine sections going south by truck. So our information in 1941 had been correct.

The observant tourist in France today may notice that almost the only bronze statuary consists of monuments to French-American notables: Washington, Franklin, Lafayette, Rochambeau. Elsewhere there are vacant pedestals. When the Germans collected all the bronze in France for their war effort, it was before the United States had entered the war and at a moment when the Hitler policy was to avoid stirring up American feelings in any way. So the "American" statuary was left. After we entered the war, the Germans evidently had so much else to do that they never got around to collecting the remaining bronze.

In mid-1941 Vichy announced that it was a crime for any French citizen to listen to the BBC, and urged all true French-men to spy on their neighbors, reporting any infraction of the new law. One evidence of the public reaction to this and other increasing Nazi pressures was that the numerous German commissions who at first swaggered around in uniform now found it prudent to dress in civilian clothes. Most of these clothes were made by French tailors, since good cloth was hard to come by in Germany. But the commissions kept coming: German naval officers, posing as Alsatians demobilized from the defeated French army, were going out with every boat to North Africa and Martinique. By autumn the Nazis were offering "high pay and liberal allowances for dependents" to volunteers for the Legion Against Bolshevism they were now forming. Despite grave unemployment in France, they found few takers. The Allied occupation of Iran had completed the circle drawn around Nazidom, and everyone, including most Germans, felt that the war had entered a new phase.

As foreigners, we were constantly aware of German watchfulness over everything we did, particularly over everything we wrote. Letters from the States sometimes bore three, and in some instances four, censors' stamps. In these latter cases the Spanish censor had added his bit of inspection to that already done by the British, the French and the Germans. The Germans were the most systematic. Each envelope bore a penciled number corresponding to that on the letter itself. Occasionally a neatly printed slip would be enclosed: "The enclosure mentioned in this letter was missing when it came into censor's hands." Different censors used different methods. Usually there were marks where the paper had been brushed with several sorts of chemical solutions, heavy pink, ocher or green stains where someone had tested the paper for invisible ink or other secret writing. At the outset of our work we thought that mail within the unoccupied zone was safe from censorship, but we soon learned that it was not. Even letters within the city of Marseilles sometimes bore unmistakable signs of having been opened for examination.

One instance of censorship cost me some uneasy moments. Arriving one day at Vernet for a visit, I was asked to go

directly to the commandant's office and there was confronted
with a letter sent me from Geneva, which I had never received.
It contained some critical remarks about the Vichy regime
and the police administration in Vernet, and instead of forwarding the letter to me the censor had sent it to the Vernet
commandant. Fortunately, I had already established good relations with the commandant, but it took some explaining that
I did not share my correspondent's sentiments, and the promise
to do what I could to correct this "misinformation" about the
camps in France before my permission to visit was renewed.
Had it not been for my previous satisfactory relations with
the commandant, this Geneva indiscretion might well have
finished my camp visitations. On another occasion one of my
letters to a rather jumpy canon in England was supposed to
have led to certain imprudent correspondence on his part
which almost resulted in the Germans' closing the Orthodox
Theological Academy in Paris.

The Vichy atmosphere depended upon the course of the
war, and this was true of the majority of Frenchmen as well,
at least for the first year after the debacle. If the Germans, as
well as the absolutely honest BBC, announced a victory for
Hitler, collaborationist stock went up. If there was good news
from the British, you could feel hope stirring in France and
hear hints that collaboration with Hitler might not be the best
policy after all. French friends in the relief agencies were extremely sensitive to Allied victories or losses, indicated by their
being more or less free to express their thoughts about the
struggle.

One thoroughly stable Frenchman, however, was an exception. His Eminence Cardinal Gerlier, ranking prelate in
southern France, had been interested in our work from the
start, had sent his personal representative to our Nîmes meetings, and had offered help in other ways. Several times he
received me in audience, when we requested his intervention
in Vichy, now apparently almost completely under Catholic
control. The old Marshal was supposed to be quite sensitive

to the Cardinal's opinions, but caught as he was between the Nazis and his Catholic conscience he could not always do what the Cardinal asked of him.

Having experienced several revolutions, I have a theory that posters are a sort of barometer of disorder: the more bills stuck up where they should not be, the nearer the approach to anarchy. In southern French cities during 1941 the posters were everywhere: the walls of all the buildings, including schools and churches, bore a coat of paper six or eight layers thick. Posters covered all lamp and telephone posts. Facing a paper shortage so severe that we had to import writing paper from Switzerland, we wondered where the material for all these broadsheets came from.

About one in five of all these public notices bore a portrait of Marshal Pétain and one or another of his solemn if somewhat inane dicta. This was only part of the intensive campaign to build an ideal picture of the Chief of the French state. Pétain, the peerless leader, who alone had been able to save France from perishing in the disaster of the year before. Both he and the press harped so much on saving their honor that one wondered at just what date honor began in the Pétain calendar. Pétain the wise, fatherly head of the state, whose most vague and vapid phrases were posted up everywhere with frames around them. For Mothers' Day the Marshal "who gives you the opportunity of celebrating" got more space in the posters than the mothers. For the Pétain version of May 1, the international labor day, the posters carried a picture of the Marshal's baton laid across an anvil and the words: "I keep promises, even those of others." This unqualified adulation was laid on with such a heavy brush that, even in the usually favorable psychological atmosphere of a people staggering under the shock of an entirely unanticipated defeat and ready to grasp at any straw of hope, it did not carry conviction. I watched the people of three different cities when Pétain made an official visit and observed that most of the "wild enthusiasm" reported in the papers was in the reporters' imaginations. And although it was still almost heresy to speak a disparaging word about the Marshal, save in the most intimate circles, more and more people, instead of mentioning the "Chief of State," began to speak of "the poor old man."

fifteen

"THE JEWISH QUESTION"

I<small>N</small> GERMANY HITLER HAD opened 1941 with a prophecy that Jews would soon be completely eliminated from Europe. Within a month a new "Commissioner General for Jewish Questions" was appointed, and the accompanying decree spelled out his duties. Out of a mass of details in the Commissioner's instructions, it appeared that all the new laws were to apply to "the whole of the national territory," thus apparently erasing any difference between the situation of Jews in occupied or unoccupied France. A few months later the Germans announced that all Jews who had entered France since January, 1936 (!), would be incorporated into work battalions and moved to concentration camps. This order applied to both occupied and unoccupied zones: it was one step nearer complete occupation of France.

One of the first echoes of this decree was the report from
Vernet that a large number of "German and other refugees"
who protested extradition to Germany or transport to North
Africa for work on the Trans-Sahara railroad had been shot.
Every refugee knew what it meant to join a labor gang on the
Trans-Sahara. The rare escapees told of conditions resembling
those of the slaves who built Pharaoh's pyramids: long hours
of toil under the desert sun, nights on the bare sand without
shelter or bedding, and the appalling lack of water. A Jewish
lawyer from Vienna who had managed to buy his way out of
one of these labor gangs but was arrested on his way to
America and forced into a labor battalion in France, told me
that the French work battalion was like a summer vacation in
the country as compared with conditions in the Sahara.

Next came a law excluding Jews from all the armed services.
Then we learned that five thousand Jews, mostly foreign, had
been arrested in the occupied zone and transferred to a labor
camp near Orléans. At the same moment in southern France
five thousand "able-bodied foreign Jews" were roused from
their beds one morning and ordered to the railroad station.
They were told to bring their luggage, including bedding and
food for twenty-four hours. After a medical examination (it
was unheard-of that any man so taken was ever declared unfit
for labor) they were moved to camps near Lorient "to be used
on public work projects." The Nazis were pushing the construction of their massive Atlantic wall, and loss of workers
by Allied bombing forced frequent new recruiting for the
hazardous job.

New laws permitted the préfet of each province to act on
his own authority in carrying out new arrests. Sixty-five Jews
living on their own resources along the Riviera were transferred to Vernet, charged with "illicit trading," and similar
reports came in from southern cities. Almost every day the
papers reported the names of French managers appointed for
Jewish concerns in northern France.

In mid-June Vichy moved further to coordinate its anti-

Semitic laws with those of Hitler, and began openly to imitate
his tactics. A "Jewish plot" to poison French-German relations by a whispering campaign was "discovered," and twelve
thousand Jews in southern France were arrested under accusation of participating in this plot. Vallat, the Commissioner for
Jewish Questions, now openly stated that he was redrafting
the laws to agree with those in "other parts of Europe." Employment for Jews was now limited to agriculture and other
manual labor, or they could be tradesmen like tailors or
jewelers. The way in which this limitation was expressed was
cynical to the extreme: at the end of a long list of businesses
and professions in which Jews were forbidden to engage came
"et cetera." This meant that the police could arrest a Jew for
any reason they chose to apply.

Jews in Vichy France were ordered "within one month" to
deposit with the police a written declaration of their "race,
religion, family connection, their professions and their possessions." Two months later, apparently basing the action on
the "possessions" declarations received, the Commissioner for
Jewish Questions was authorized to sell all property belonging
to Jews. This legalized the transfer to non-Jewish hands of
all Jewish property in southern France. Earlier restrictions
had been applied chiefly to foreign Jews, now that distinction
was to disappear. Not even Jewish war veterans were exempt
from the new larceny. Vichy reported that "Aryanization"
was proceeding well: all Jewish firms now had "managers"
assigned to them.

Anyone not usefully employed risked automatic transfer
to the German-controlled labor battalions. To these groups
the police now began to transfer all "able-bodied men between fourteen and sixty-five, regardless of their nationality."
All our relief agencies were excluded from camps while the
German control commission carried out its operation, and
when we were again admitted most of the male refugees had
disappeared. Quotas for Jews in the universities were now
announced. Only 3 per cent of students in a given school could

be Jewish and only 2 per cent of these would be permitted to study medicine.

Soon after this, while Berlin had begun to admit "a shortage of labor due to the war" and was forbidding any Jew to leave the Reich, Heydrich was doing the same in what had once been Czechoslovakia: Jews must wear the yellow star of David and remain in the country. Vichy moved to "eliminate all Jewish influence from the national economy"; French "managers" of Jewish enterprises were authorized to sell them, except in the case of residential property. Proceeds were to be deposited in a "Jewish Fund," after a 10 per cent handling charge had been deducted. The Fund was to be used, Vichy claimed, "to aid destitute Jews" manufactured by this very edict. It was typical of anti-Semitic Vichy tactics that the execution of this decree was left to the discretion of the Commissioner for Jewish Questions. In other words, not every Jewish businessman would be stripped of his possessions. No better way to arouse jealousy and dissension among French Jews could have been devised.

A prominent rabbi wrote a protest to Vichy, and received this reply: "You quote a number of French writers in your protest. These would never have been contradicted by French legislation if it were not for many Jews who have invaded our country during the last few years, who have absolutely no ties with our civilization. I will not try to refute the statistics you cite about Jews who fought and died for France. This is a matter deserving too much reverence to be the object of controversy. I must say, however, that in this Government's attitude there is no anti-Semitism, but only the consideration of the supreme interests of the State."

Early in September Vichy papers reported that in Paris one hundred of the country's most prominent Jews had been arrested. The German order justified itself by citing "the suffering in a war forced on Germany by the Jewry of other countries." Among those jailed was the prominent philanthropist David Weill, one of France's leading art collectors.

His gifts to the Louvre were widely known, and most friends
of art knew he had provided the funds for removal to safety
in Geneva of the treasures of the Prado, threatened by the
Spanish civil war.

The hundred Jews arrested at this time were "held responsible for public order," which in plain language meant
that they were hostages. In Germany the war stresses began
to increase. Hitler called on the German people for further
sacrifices in a war against "Jewish capitalism and Bolshevism
united to destroy the Reich." A New York *Times* editorial
remarked that the Jews were condemned as conspiring (a) to
corner the world's capital and (b) to destroy it: "The Führer
is not handicapped by such a triviality as logic."

On October 1, 1941, Vichy solemnly announced that "the
Council of Ministers today approved the draft of a law fixing
the status of Jews in France." Word was permitted to leak out
that new categories were to be set up. French Jews who had
served in the army would have more privileges (or less restrictions!) than others. "Foreign Jews newly arrived in
France have no professional or other privileges."

From German cities now crumbling under Allied bombing
came reports of mass evacuations of Jews from their apart-
ments, in order to shelter bombed-out Aryans. Jews were
being moved to temporary shelters outside the cities, before
being transported to Poland. The papers advertised the sale
of household and personal effects of prosperous Jewish homes
so cleared: linen, clothing, carpets, silverware—articles almost
impossible to purchase elsewhere, even with ration cards. A
pamphlet published at the time warned Germans to "remember
that every Jew is your enemy. Every German aiding a Jew
commits treason." Apparently just awakening to the facts,
the New York *Times* commented: "The complete elimination
of Jews from European life now appears to be German
policy." Jews were classified as "criminals," "undesirable
social elements."

Echoing the Berlin orders, Vichy again "recodified" its

anti-Jewish laws. All Jews must now join the "General Union of Israelites." The new organization was responsible for all relations with the government. All Jews must contribute "according to their means" to this organization, which replaced all other Jewish organizations now dissolved, and their property would be transferred to the Union. Religious organizations were exempt (only temporarily, as it developed) from this decree. All the property of the Union was placed under the control of the "General Commissioner for Jewish Questions."

Vichy seemed still a few paces behind the anti-Semitism of occupied territory, and consequently there were renewed attempts by Jews to cross the demarcation line into southern France. Vichy ordered all provincial governors to tighten the border lines; to increase the number of guards and take more severe measures, including "administrative internment," against Jews attempting to flee the occupied zone. Newspapers published lists of those imprisoned for attempting to cross the line.

But despite the now closely guarded demarcation line, the flow of Jews, and particularly Jewish children, into southern France was steadily increasing. By early summer all the children's colonies and homes operated by the Nîmes Committee organizations were crowded to capacity. And more kept coming, with or without the help of our agencies. In one fortnight two hundred children came across, little groups acting on their own initiative, finding holes in the line of demarcation. One boy of ten was brought by his parents to the line and sent across alone, since the father, a prominent Jew, dared not risk the consequences if he should be caught in an attempt to pass into southern France. The boy walked several miles at night and turned up at a farmhouse in unoccupied territory the next morning. The OSE found shelter for the lad in one of their Marseilles homes.

Even before deportation from southern France began, our Nîmes agencies had been at work, usually with reluctant consent from Vichy, removing children from camps into homes or colonies—like Vence for the Czechoslovaks—organized to receive them. This was not as simple as it sounds. Each case precipitated a family crisis. After the years of suffering together, should a family now be separated? Most parents tried to convince themselves that this was only a temporary separation, and sending their children to well-organized homes set up by the different agencies was so manifestly the right thing to do that in the end few parents refused to make the decision. They could not know then that, in most cases, this meant the salvation of these youngsters from the general deportations which occurred later.

By the summer of 1941 practically all our organizations were engaged in various efforts to help Jews escape the Vichy police. Clandestine passage into Switzerland was one way: later, when I was visiting refugee camps in Switzerland I frequently met Jewish friends I had first known in French camps. They had survived the hazardous adventure, with the help of Catholics and Protestants who had served as guides and "passers."

Quite understandably, the Swiss were not giving visas to people unable to produce evidence that they could eventually travel further, and who might thus become public charges in Switzerland. Hence any person we assisted to bypass the French border police had to have a visa in his passport indicating that he could travel to some overseas country. I do not recall that we ever forged United States visas, but one way to assist Jews to enter Switzerland was to place a Cambodian or a Portuguese or a Mexican visa on their passports. Soon several of our agencies were engaged in forgery.

The Czech Aid office was a good example. We had a few specialists in consular signatures. One man could make a perfect imitation of the signature of the Mexican attaché responsible for issuing visas; another practiced for weeks to be able to forge the name of the Portuguese consul general. This was a somewhat risky procedure, although the counterfeit signature would be seen only by border police. Since all our exported men were going to Britain, the "imitation" visas could harm no one, and they worked perfectly when we had to use them.

An amusing incident occurred with regard to the Portuguese consul's signature. After my Czech friend had reproduced this autograph on some scores of passports, he was astounded one day to receive a letter from the gentleman in question himself, with his own bona fide signature. It turned out that a French friend of Czech Aid had told the Portuguese consul about our farms, suggesting that he write and ask for help in feeding his family.

If legal or semilegal entry into Switzerland was impossible, the only other way was to cross the borderline at some unguarded place in the mountains. Before the Germans occupied the whole of France, the French side of the border was not too heavily guarded, and study of the habits of the Swiss frontier police would indicate that at certain times of the day some spot on the borderline would be unwatched. This type of escape was much easier to read about than to attempt, and as winter drew on it became a terrible ordeal, particularly for elderly people. Some could not endure it.

Although some fugitives stopped by the Swiss border police were refused entrance, it stands to the eternal credit of the Swiss people that once the whole of France was occupied a refugee who had actually passed the border and was within the country was never refused asylum.

And as with our Czech veterans, if you could not export them you had to hide them. Already, all over unoccupied France, Jews were seeking places of concealment. Here a Catholic institution, there a Protestant village, the Christian forces joined in efforts to keep these hunted people from the police.

In Marseilles the prior of a Dominican monastery turned his house into a city of refuge. Here passports were forged, predated certificates of baptism were fabricated. (I knew a prominent Jewish woman who held two baptismal certificates, one Protestant and one Catholic. Happily, she survived the war.) Through his Catholic connections the good prior could arrange, even after the German occupation, to pass his "clients" into the Italian occupied zone and thence into Italy, where, despite the official declarations, actual cases of Jewish persecution were far less frequent than in Nazi territory. When finally the Gestapo came to arrest the prior, he received them in his sitting room, excused himself "to pick up a rosary," and never came back.

Never before in normally law-abiding France had there been such widespread, well-organized disobedience to police regulations. The police, after all, were Frenchmen, and their fellow citizens were shocked that this inhuman treatment of foreigners was being carried out by Frenchmen in a country which once had led the world in defense of the rights of man. It was the sort of thing we had come to expect from the Nazis, but to have the honor of France thus dragged in the mire was unforeseen tragedy. In numerous cases policemen resigned in protest: it was no light matter for a man with a family to give up his job in these near-starvation times.

To their protests French Christians added action. One of my friends, a Catholic priest, was arrested because he refused to reveal the hiding place of forty children who had been stolen from under the very noses of the Vichy police. A pro-Pétain newspaper complained: "Every Catholic family is sheltering a Jew. French authorities supply them with false identity cards and passports. Priests assist them to cross into Switzerland. Jewish children are hidden in Catholic schools. Catholic officials give advance notice to Jews scheduled for deportation, so that half of them escape."

That Vichy paper told only part of the truth. All Christian forces, Protestant as well as Catholic, institutions as well as families, took up the cause. Jews who had escaped from camp, or now no longer dared to live in freedom, would be sheltered by a convent, a convalescent home or a Protestant village.

This nationwide conspiracy to confound and circumvent

the occupying army was possible because of the magnificent teamwork of Christians, both Catholic and Protestant. It was like the underground railroad of pre-Civil War days. Small groups of refugees were escorted, almost always by night, from station to station toward the Swiss border. For a time the groups were turned over to professional "passers" for the arduous and dangerous crossing of the frontier line, members of the Nîmes Committee paying the very considerable fee these smugglers charged. Later the task became so dangerous that the professionals retired from business and our amateurs had to carry on. Not once, but time and again, the Christian guide was arrested by the border police—fortunately the French rather than the Germans—and was jailed for a month, the customary penalty for smuggling. As the war went on, the Germans were unable to watch the Swiss frontier as meticulously as formerly (although they now used dogs), which made it easier for the amateur passers.

One by one the non-French men in Jewish organizations began to disappear. They had not left their posts voluntarily: they had simply been started on the way to Auschwitz as a result of what sometimes seemed like reckless courage. Not one of these men engaged in succoring refugees in camps would have been unable to escape from France if he had so desired. The apparatus for safe passage into Switzerland was always at their disposal. However, they saw their duty clearly and paid the tragic price for doing it. One of the veteran leaders wrote me from the children's home he was managing and said that this letter would probably be the last I would receive from him. It was.

sixteen

WINE
ON RATION CARDS

Meanwhile the condition of all refugees, Jews or not, worsened as Vichy France came more completely under German control. In the spring of '41 new cuts in rations were announced: seven ounces of bread per day—for a people whose every menu was built around bread—and relief workers were reporting to the American Red Cross that, unless outside help should come, this would be reduced to four and a half ounces in the summer. Meat, including horse meat, at one and a quarter ounces per person could not be sold on the three meatless days per week, and each citizen was allowed two and a third pounds per month, with a pound of fats and a half pound of cheese to back it up. Poor harvests and bungling administration might be blamed for the shortages, but everyone knew that the main reason was Germany. As one of my French friends put it, "The barter arrangement we have with the Germans is wonderful: we give them our wheat, and in exchange they take our coal." French humor helped save many situations, but behind this was anger at the sight of trainloads of food supplies headed for Germany.

Division of France into two parts by the demarcation line was another reason for the shortages. In general, southern France was a land of vineyards, while the great wheat-growing regions were all in the north. So now Toulouse, never self-sufficient in grain production, had to skimp to share with the Riviera, which produced more carnations than grapes. Potatoes, that staple of poverty-stricken countries, grew only in the north, and for months on end in Marseilles we never saw a potato. Even in midsummer fresh vegetables were rationed at a half pound per person per day.

Food shortages affected the children most of all. You would see them in cold schoolrooms, wearing outdoor wraps, shawls or scarves over their black school aprons. Most of them would have no food from breakfast until they returned home in the late afternoon. Here the American Friends Service Committee undertook one of their largest operations, providing a "gouter," or midafternoon snack, for nearly a half million school children in the larger cities. Like the Service Suisse, the Friends imported from Portugal or Switzerland the foods needed to maintain this program—dried fruits and vegetables, rice and cocoa. In addition, ten thousand undernourished infants received milk or baby food.

As in every other war-torn country, the shortages meant that housewives had to spend hours every day in long queues in front of food shops. In Marseilles people coming out of the late cinema on Saturday night simply moved over to "their" food store and got in line for the Sunday morning opening. The day after a shipment of eggs was received from North Africa, one such queue held over a thousand persons, waiting grimly, smiles as scarce as chocolate, hoping the supply would hold out. And if French citizens were thus restricted, foreigners still in the camps felt the pinch even more severely. Food rations were shortened. Camp doctors could examine the sick but had no medicines to give them. Thousands of camp internees had the "right" to leave, some with visas for America, some with funds sufficient for living outside camp. But all these cases had to be decided in Vichy, and the small refugee offices there were flooded by the demands.

Thanks to food purchased in Lisbon and sent us by friends, we could take a fairly normal box lunch if we went on a train journey, and then we would be ashamed to open it because probably most of the other passengers in the compartment were hungry. A French friend spoke his mind to me about the Allied broadcasts. Although it had just been declared illegal to listen to the Voice of America, he had evidently disobeyed the law: "You are always talking of your plans for reconstruction, of your stocks of food for the day after victory. But we are being jailed or shot today; our children are dying of hunger today. Winter is coming, a specter of death; our barns and cellars are empty and the enemy will leave us only what he does not want himself. What comfort is it to hear you have storehouses bursting with food for after V-day? Every year your victory is postponed for another year, and you are not in a hurry, for time is going to wear out the Germans. But we are afraid we will be worn out first."

In the early spring of '41 Vichy had introduced the new "national" footwear. We already had "national" coffee, which was coffee in name only, some shoddy "national" textiles, and now "national" shoes. These had wooden soles, producing a new clicking sound as ladies passed on the sidewalk.

Hotels posted warnings to guests not to set their shoes outside their doors at night as was the immemorial habit in European hotels, since shoes seemed to walk away by themselves. In the trains travelers leaving their seats to go to the diner prudently chained and padlocked their bags to the baggage rack, as we used to do in the years just after World War I.

With every month travel became more difficult and time-consuming. Returning one day from Geneva to Marseilles, I was fortunate in having a sleeper until 3:00 A.M., when I had to move into a day-coach and stand in an unheated corridor until 6:30, when we pulled into Marseilles. During these last hours I was comforted by the thought that most of my fellow shiverers had been standing there all night. On one trip to visit our Czechoslovak farms it would have taken fifteen hours to travel thirty-five miles by rail had I not been fortunate enough to find a charcoal-burning taxi.

Finding a taxi, even in cities like Marseilles, was no easy business. At every taxi stand there was always an eager group of would-be passengers around every machine (all of them ran on charcoal or acetylene) quarreling about who had asked the driver first, each pleading that he be accepted instead of the others. One day I was helped to secure a taxi by one of our Czech colleagues who had accompanied me to the St. Charles railroad station. My friend flourished some sort of document proving his right to priority in taxi service. The document bore an impressive seal and my signature as president of the Czechoslovak Aid. I hadn't thought of making this type of certificate for myself.

If actual travel was incommodious, getting permission to travel was more so. Here are some lines from a letter I wrote from Marseilles early in 1941. "I am suddenly called to a conference in Geneva and so I need not only an exit visa, but the permission to return here—a round-trip ticket, so to speak. I spent most of this morning in the prefecture or Government House, putting in my request (and at that I had special treatment and was able to finish in one session). A telegram, for which I paid, has gone to Vichy and now I am at the headquarters of the police to have myself looked over from the political and criminal viewpoints. It is a dirty little office with one small soiled window, partly obscured by someone's black overcoat hanging on the latch. There is one tired-looking official with his hat on, at a table in the corner by the window. Along the side of the room opposite him is a bench and on the bench is seated a miscellaneous collection of men and women, all of them evidently foreigners like myself. The official calls each in his turn and laboriously writes down their replies to all his questions. You have to account for almost every day since you were born, but especially since you came into France. You must give the names of parents and other relatives, explain all your activities while you have been here and, in general, answer any questions about your personal life and history which it may occur to this person to ask.

"I am twelfth in line. The head is occupied by a tall thin chap and a Jewish girl. She interprets for him, since he speaks no French. He has been a Polish officer here in France, having come via Hungary and Italy after the collapse of Poland. And he wants to go to Mexico. After he is finished off, the chestnut-haired girl presents her own case. She has an aunt in Wisconsin and is getting ready to go there. Now, there is a gray-haired couple, German-Poles. The official is good-humored. Kokoshin is a town in Poland: who occupies it now? The poor people who used to live there and now want to go somewhere else than France don't know. 'But we have to know,' the official explains, for the request must go to one or another department depending on which foreign government is concerned. They finally 'guess' that their village is occupied by Germans and the inquiry goes on.

"Most of the fifteen men in the room are smoking, and French tobacco at that. The only ventilation comes when the door into the corridor lets someone in or out, and the atmosphere is getting a bit heavy, but perhaps it makes waiting easier: it calms the nerves. Every little while the door opens to admit some new callers who are advised to come next week. Most of them accept the counsel and retire. There are special cases, however. Here is a draggled-looking couple come to search for their documents, seized in a police raid night before last. A while ago there was an old Frenchman who wanted permission to visit Italy. He was directed to the Government House. 'Will they give me permission there?' he insisted. 'That is their business,' the official replied and the visitor had to be content with that.

" 'You were interned at the camp at Gurs—why?' 'Why are you at liberty now?' 'How did you have permission to come to Marseilles?' 'Have you passed before the German control commission?' 'Why do you want to go to Brazil?' 'Your Spanish passport has expired. You are going to South America by sea, and not across Spain?' 'But your Mexican visa has expired.' 'Yes, but there is a certificate from the Mexican consul that we can have another.' Remarks like this drift across the room on the sea of tobacco smoke.

"Some Spaniards come in and sit down, a line of Goya-esque figures against the wall. Their wives and shaggy-headed children have been left standing in the corridor. Occasionally one of the men needs to have his wife's signature or something else for the police inquisitor, and he calls her in. Otherwise the black-shawled womenfolk remain at a respectful distance. All these unfortunate people live for only one thing: to get away from here to some other part of the globe. Here, or in their own homes, life is impossible for them—no civic rights, no work, no bread.

"My own turn came at last, after just three and one half hours of waiting. My case was simple. First of all, I was an American with a valid passport; second, I had had but three addresses during my eight years in France—Paris, Pau and Marseilles. I filled out and signed a long questionnaire which included these wartime items: 'The undersigned declares upon his honor that he will maintain the most complete secrecy about movements of airplanes or ships, about the results of bombardments or the movements of troops which he may have been able to observe on this trip. He solemnly declares that he is carrying neither arms, nor munitions, photographic apparatus, poison or carrier pigeons.' The police official said he would push the inquiry and make a report within forty-eight hours.

After that, the request has to go to Vichy and after Vichy gives permission and I have my return visa for France, I may ask for a Swiss visa. The process will take a week at least, and that is almost record time."

We were fortunate that our room was in the Terminus Hotel connected with the railroad, and in consequence had hot water three times a week, while ordinary citizens in town had it twice a month. One of our most appreciated gestures of hospitality was when we invited friends to share the bathroom on "hot water days." Morning "coffee" in the hotel was served without milk or sugar, but the saccharin tablet in the saucer was supposed to give flavor, if the sugar box in your pocket was empty. Jam was available if you wanted it, but it was made of grape sugar, hard on both teeth and digestion. In a dining car the printed menu read: "mixture replacing coffee," and it tasted just like that.

In the restaurants there was always someone haggling with the waiter over meal tickets. The ration card allowed for meat thirteen days in the month, but whole months would go by with meat coupons intact—there was no meat to be had. After a Frenchman's bread had been reduced to a few ounces a day, nothing so stunned him as having to take his wine in carefully rationed doses. Men were allowed four cigarettes per day; women had none. It was surprising how many friends the nonsmoking men discovered among their smoker acquaintances. At a wedding "banquet" in our hotel I watched the vice-mayor of the city clearing out the ashtrays as we rose from the table, and putting the butts into a little case he carried for that purpose.

Actually these steadily increasing restrictions helped bring the average Frenchman out of the shock of the debacle. Wine shortage was something for which he could not blame the British blockade. The man in the street began to see that Britain was right in tightening the blockade, even if it forced the Germans to take more and more out of France. One of my neighbors remarked, "The more we hear of collaboration the less we have to eat. If this is the 'organization' of Europe, I'd prefer disorganization." Some people claimed that the Germans were starving the cities to incite raids on villages by hungry city folk, thus providing a pretext for total German occupation. Many now were doubting an ultimate German victory.

Censorship was intensified. The editor of a paper said: "You should believe nothing we print except the notices of births and deaths and weddings." Although listening to foreign radio was forbidden, people believed far more in the BBC than in their own radio and press, and many were beginning to listen to the appeals of de Gaulle. Every town saw some of its factories closed and the workers obliged to "volunteer" for factory work in the Reich. By autumn 1941 the resistance movement was well organized, and most of us were somehow engaged in it. "Export" operations for Frenchmen were intensified; "cells" à la Lenin were organized. It was only after the war that I learned the name of the "network" to which our "cell" belonged. Certain of the leaders were sent abroad and the rest assigned to tasks at home. A "retired" lawyer from Paris, now living as a peasant on his small farm near Nîmes, was a way station for clandestine passage of men or news or orders. A pastor's apartment in Marseilles was constantly in use to hide escapees from the north until false documents could be prepared for them, and among the best forgers of passports and other documents in southern France were two Protestant pastors. Catholic and Protestant clerics collaborated in the most effective of a dozen "underground" resistance papers.

The distribution of these clandestine papers would have been much more difficult without the tacit support of at least some of the authorities. In particular, some of the police were already sympathetic with the Resistance movement. When I arrived at the office in the morning, stepping over the frowsy alcoholic who regularly used the tiled stairs as a bedroom, I might find a mimeographed sheet tucked under the door—a "Message from General de Gaulle," or news of some recent German atrocity. A similar sheet might be left on the seats in a train or pasted over a Pétain poster on a hoarding.

One striking thing about the Resistance effort was the complete and sympathetic collaboration not only of Catholics and Protestants but of Christians with Communists. Communist agencies for underground action were in existence in France before the debacle, and of course could carry on undisturbed afterward. All the Communist know-how and, so far as we could learn, most of their organization was placed at the disposal of the Resistance leaders, whether Christian, Jew or Communist. And with some of France's best authors— Malraux, for example—actively participating, some of the underground literature turned out to be excellent French writing.

In the first months following the collapse of France and the German occupation, many Frenchmen, too stunned to pass objective judgment, had agreed with Pétain: "After all we have heard about Nazi frightfulness, it is surprising what gentlemanly treatment they are giving us." Now that naive optimism began to fade. With each new hint of French resistance the German reaction became more violent. Some of the news about these moves was printed in official publications, but there were also waves of rumor: fifty hostages shot in retaliation for the killing of two German officers; a young Frenchman executed in Nantes for allegedly abetting the escape of prisoners of war to the unoccupied zone. Active resistance and the mood to resist increased in intensity. Under enemy occupation protest is dangerous, but people found ways to express it.

When the Germans in Paris put up posters announcing that a French officer had been shot for "resisting a German policeman" the public was impressed, but not in the way intended. At once groups of men and women appeared, and remained kneeling before the posters. In some places the crowd was so great it disrupted traffic, and eventually the occupying forces had to remove the placards.

In Marseilles the morning after the Yugoslavs had thrown out the collaborationist Prince Paul, enthroned the young King Peter and declared war on Germany, Helen passed the place on the Cannebière where a plaque between the tram tracks marked the spot of King Alexander's assassination in 1934. Someone had laid a tiny bunch of flowers on the plaque. Helen went on to the office and came back with a large bouquet someone had given her and placed it beside the first flower tribute. That started a city-wide demonstration. More and more flowers were brought until there was a drift of blossoms thirty feet long between the tracks. The police finally barred all pedestrians from access to the place. After that people would board a tram and drop their flowers as they passed the spot. A parallel demonstration occurred at the Alexander-Barthou monument, ceasing only when the police closed all the florist shops in the city.

During these abnormal times Marseilles, Queen of the Mediterranean, presented an outwardly normal face. Along the sun-bathed streets there were still cafés under the plane trees; carefree-looking people filled the tables at any hour of the day or night (in most of the better cafés ration cards for wine were not demanded; you simply paid the waiter a double tip); barefoot itinerant boy bootblacks solicited customers; coffee-colored hawkers of North African rugs (sometimes dispensing heroin as well) moved through the crowds, each with a pile of his wares over one shoulder and strings of vari-colored beads looped over his arm. Save for the divers military uniforms, and of these fewer and fewer were being worn, the ancient city looked as it always had. You might see a shuffling file of manacled prisoners under police escort, perhaps headed for Vernet, or a double rank of children, hand in hand, with two brown-robed nuns at the head of the procession, on their way to the Botanical Garden.

Up in the "old Town," where the steep cramped streets

had been a refuge for fugitives from justice or from oppression since time immemorial, a discarded German uniform might be seen in the gutter any early morning. Whether its owner had shed it voluntarily as a deserter from Hitler's army or whether he had been "liquidated" by some agent of the Resistance there was no way of knowing.

seventeen

VISAS

FOR APATRIDES

Among the new words re-
sulting from the war, like "jeep" or "commando," we relief
agencies found ourselves constantly using the French word
"apatride," no matter what language we were speaking.
"Displaced persons" was a term that appeared only after the
war.

Apatrides were the thousands who had no passports, what
they had when they left home having been declared invalid
by the powers now occupying their homelands: Spaniards
or Germans or Czechs now disowned by the governments in
power. Apatride means man without a country. Most of our
refugees had become men without a continent, and most of
them were trying to leave Europe for some other part of
the globe.

Whether or not you have a country you must have some
sort of document proving that you are you. Even in peacetime,
one of the gravest accidents that can befall a traveler is to lose
his passport, and even if he never left home no European
would think of living without an identity card. The story
went around Paris of the Ukrainian refugee who decided to
end her troubles by jumping into the Seine. Having arrived
at the bridge, she changed her mind and dropped her carte
d'identité into the water instead.

Even where there were no legal obstacles, most refugees
found it very difficult to obtain or renew their identity cards.
The police insisted upon the usual fee for all cases. That
spring of 1941 one of our Jewish agencies was writing to
New York: "The préfets refuse to consider the poverty of
applicants. We have adopted the method of having all single
men enlist in work groups, thus avoiding the expense of
identity cards. Can we take the responsibility of doing the
same for married men? We feel that families should not be
separated." Refugees in camp were adversity personified, but
those at liberty faced problems as well. If they admitted to
the police that they were penniless, this meant joining the
thousands already in Gurs or other camps. Foreigners without
visible means of support, they lived in a constant state of
dread: every action had to be weighed under the shadow of
possible internment. The request for an identity card or a
travel permit involved contact with the police and thus
exposure of their vulnerable positions.

Along with "apatride," probably no other word was used
more often than "visa." Every refugee hoped to leave for
some less dangerous place. To move anywhere, a set of visas
on one's passport was necessary. Regulations governing visas
varied with the months, the type of refugee, and the changing
military and political scene. At one moment you could not
obtain a French exit permit until you had all the other visas
lined up and in your passport. But most consulates would not
issue transit visas before the refugee could present a steamer

reservation: Portugal and Spain were taking no chances on having more refugees stranded in their territory. On the other hand, the few steamship lines in operation hesitated to reserve a place until the visas in a would-be passenger's passport proved that he really could reach the port of departure. Everyone talked of visas: every organization was more or less engaged in helping refugees obtain them, sometimes facing quite unpredictable complications. The Quakers worked for two years on a visa for one Fritz Schmidt and the Emergency Rescue Committee spent an equal amount of time on one Theodore Schmidt, before they discovered that the two names represented the same person.

Generally the cooperation among our agencies was better coordinated. Cooperation was often dictated by circumstances. Most agencies were limited in the amount of money they might use for a given refugee, and in scores of cases the given refugee needed twice or three times that amount. Here two or three organizations would join funds to enable the person in question to get out of France.

Failure to secure the right visas at the right time could mean death in an extermination camp in Poland. Frustration followed frustration: refugees suffered nervous collapse, unable to endure the tension. On occasion the usual esprit de corps among refugees failed. The Rescue Committee had moved heaven and earth to secure a U.S. "danger visa" for one Joseph Braun, internee in Gurs. The camp authorities alerted another Joseph Braun who calmly accepted the visa and went off to America. The right Joseph Braun discovered this only after the other was safely out of France.

There were legal and not-so-legal ways of procuring visas. Certain consulates might be "persuaded" to bypass the regulations. In rare cases a personal appeal to the authority concerned would procure the necessary rubber-stamped note in an endangered man's passport. One such personal connection with the consul of a certain Southeast Asian country was most useful. And the records must show the names of scores of immigrants to that far-off land, who never got farther than the Free French forces in North Africa or Britain.

"Aryans" could obtain exit permits from France much more easily than Jews, though the latter formed the overwhelming majority of the refugee population. Early in 1941 Vichy had appealed to the United States to accept a larger number of refugees from southern France, to which our State Department replied that one way Vichy could reduce the number of refugees there would be to grant exit permits to the hundreds of persons who already had United States immigration visas.

Of these, at least 90 per cent were Jewish. The Macher case was typical. Interned in Vernet, Macher had received a "convocation" from the American consulate in Marseilles, indicating that a United States visa was awaiting him there. Macher put in the proper written request for permission to travel to Marseilles to receive the visa. After weeks without a reply, the American consulate wrote Macher again. Again he requested a travel permit, but as an internee that was all he could do. After this happened a third time, a lawyer acting on behalf of the Coordination Committee called on the Vernet commandant to inquire. He learned that Macher's request, after reposing for months on the commandant's desk, had been forwarded to the Commissariat for Jewish Affairs in Paris. It might as well have been referred to Rosenberg himself.

One day the Czech Aid office received from the American consulate a list of thirty-two names—Czechoslovak citizens who had been granted entry visas into the United States. This was evidently part of a scheme to move as many Czechs as possible out of the Germans' reach, so they could join their own armed forces in Britain. Of the whole list, not one man was known to any Czechoslovak agency in southern France. In any case these men would go to England, not to America, so after we had some discussion in the office, thirty-two men living at La Blancherie were renamed and provided

with the proper identity papers. Thus thirty-two more
Czechs were able to reach England and continue the battle
against Hitler.

By this time the Czech Aid office possessed an excellent set
of "official" consular and police stamps and could arrange
almost any man's papers for departure or change of residence.
Certain Czech passports could not pass German-sympathizing
border police in Spain, for instance. Even in peacetime, in
some well-authenticated cases where a passport had been lost,
the Prefecture would issue a substitute document "in lieu of
a passport," on which the holder could have consular visas
affixed. With the collaboration of friends in the Prefecture
office, these blanks could be had, after which it was a simple
matter to fill them in and affix the "official" stamp. Then a
Spanish and a Portuguese transit visa would be stamped on
the document, together with a destination visa. Since some
Czechs had actually emigrated to Venezuela, this was the
destination usually indicated.

There were occasions, however, when the lack of a visa
proved useful. After the American head of the Emergency
Rescue Committee had been engaged for more than a year
in his "nefarious" efforts to save the lives of imperiled intellectuals, under ever closer surveillance by the police, he was
finally arrested and taken to the Spanish frontier at Cerbère
for deportation. But he had no Spanish visa in his passport,
and so he was able to remain in France several months more.

Of all the organizations concerned with emigration, none
had a more romantic story than the Emergency Rescue
Committee, later known as the American Rescue Committee.
Concerned with the fate of German Socialists and members
of other liberal groups after France was overrun, the Committee set up an office in Marseilles, with the avowed intention
of aiding these well-known leaders to escape by any means
possible. This purpose was no secret to the police, but the
Committee was permitted to operate long enough to move
scores of "wanted" refugees to safety. Many of the most

famous names in European liberal circles profited by its ministrations. Based on the State Department's authorization of emergency visas outside the normal quota system, the Rescue Committee could help special refugees to obtain such, and then supply the material aid necessary for travel to safety.

Here was a prominent Hungarian journalist, living in Switzerland at the outbreak of war and editing an anti-Nazi paper. He moved at once to France and volunteered in the only military unit available, the French Foreign Legion. Twice decorated, he was taken prisoner by the Germans, who did not discover his identity before he escaped and arrived in Marseilles. For many refugees a visa to some Latin-American country was the simplest and speediest way out, but these countries did not recognize the visas of stateless persons, apatrides: they required a national passport. In this particular case the passport was still valid but it had to be amended, since it authorized travel "in European countries" only. However, the minute this passport came into a Hungarian consul's hands it would be confiscated. Thanks to the Rescue Committee, a U.S. emergency visa was issued on a separate travel document; the journalist could use his Hungarian passport for Spain and Portugal, and take a ship in Lisbon.

Leon Feuchtwanger, bound for a deportation camp, was snatched from a stumbling line of refugees by "unknown persons" in a passing car. Thanks to one of the refugee agencies he was able to cross the Pyrenees on foot, dressed as a woman. To avoid further perilous delay he used the steamer reservation of the head of another agency, and so was able to reach the States safely.

In some cases, along with the tragedy, there was humor. Franz Werfel had left Paris at the time of the exodus, and was living in Lourdes when Martha Sharp and Helen Lowrie, representing the Unitarian Service Committee, called on him. Out of this contact, incidentally, came *The Song of Bernadette*: although Werfel had been living in Lourdes for weeks, he had never visited the famous shrine, and the two ladies took him to see it. His interest aroused, Werfel produced the book after he reached the States. But getting there was no easy matter. American visas were available, and Werfel and his wife moved to Marseilles. With the help of the Rescue Committee false passports were provided, since France was too friendly with Hitler to let such a prominent Jew pass through Spain. For months the Werfels sat in a hotel, hoping for some legal means of emigration and fearing to attempt anything clandestine. At last they realized there was no other way, and agreed to let the Rescue Committee engage a guide to take them over the mountains at the frontier near Perpignan. If anything clandestine was ever less secret, we never heard of it. The lady refused to attempt the passage at night, and appeared for the hike over the mountains in bright sunlight; wearing a white dress and carrying a white parasol, she was about as inconspicuous as a fly in a glass of milk. Frontier guards had evidently been "approached," however, and the Werfels came safely to the States.

Probably 90 per cent of all refugees wanted to go to the United States. Obtaining an American visa was often a time-consuming process, and under the shadow of imminent German occupation haste was essential. A refugee had to present three affidavits of support from three separate persons. It not infrequently happened that two would arrive, but the third would be missing, so correspondence with the States had to be renewed to secure that third affidavit. By this time the steamship reservation might be useless, and then negotiation would have to take place all over again.

There was one prominent writer who had managed to reach Morocco and who possessed a U.S. visa. It took him months to secure permission to move to Tangier, where he had his steamer reservation. While he waited, the U.S. visa expired, but the consulate in Morocco extended it. In Tangier, however, the U.S. consul felt the need of new instructions from Washington and in the meantime our friend missed his boat. Again the visa expired. This man's danger was heightened by new events in France, and finally the Rescue Committee gave up hope and helped the man obtain a visa for Cuba. It is pleasant to report that he eventually reached the promised land in New York.

The case of Professor B. was another excellent example of visa complications. Through one of the agencies U.S. visas and passage for the professor and his wife were guaranteed, but it took a month to secure the Portuguese transit visa: only in Lisbon could he obtain steamer reservations. The U.S. visa expired. Overanxious, Professor B. alerted two organizations, and both submitted his case to the State Department. Once this confusion was cleared, the Department cabled the visa to Nice, but Professor B. had already moved to Marseilles. Transferring the visa to Marseilles caused a delay of a few more weeks, but finally the Bs got off on the SS *Winnipeg*, which sailed as far as Trinidad where the French detained it until the visas had again expired.

Further correspondence moved Washington to renew the visa a second time, and eight weeks later it came, but it mentioned only Professor B. and not his wife. So the Bs had to go through the whole process again. A letter to B. from the Rescue Committee explained that "One reason for the delay is that your case was recommended by Professor R. who is thought to have Communist leanings." Two months later the Rescue Committee was writing: "The next step is a statement about your and your wife's relatives: who are dead, where the others are living, if in Germany, what contacts, if any, you have with them, etc. The statement is to be furnished in triplicate with two of the copies notarized." These extracts from correspondence tell the rest of the story.

September—"The American consul in Trinidad has received no instructions about the Bs."

October—"Learned that State Department has disapproved the Bs' visa. There is no explanation."

December—"The Bs decided to ask for a Cuban visa. Sponsors must provide new biographical material."

January—"The Enemy Alien Act rules that no one of enemy nationality may receive a visa or an extension of one."

March—"We hope to find someone to present the Bs' appeal in Washington."

June—"Very difficult to find anyone to push Bs' appeal for reconsideration."

August—"The Bs' case will be heard on August 17."

November—"This case refused after hearing."

There is a final happy note in this file: "June 27, 1945. The Bs arrived in New York."

For many of these hunted people the expiration date of a visa was almost like a date for execution. Some years after the war, in New York, I met an ex-refugee who greeted me with "You saved my life." I had no recollection of the case, but this man explained: "I was in the army and could not reach Marseilles before my American visa expired. The American consulate was refusing to receive people like me, but you gave me a note to the consul and I was able to take a ship for New York."

On the other hand, there was Dr. H., another prominent Jewish writer on the Nazis' "wanted" list. He came into my office one afternoon. "But I thought you had left on yesterday's boat," I said. "I was aboard the ship," he replied, "and as you know my U.S. visa would expire at midnight. The police knew it, too, but since our ship was to sail at 10:00 P.M., they did nothing. Then there was some delay with loading, and after midnight the harbor police took me off. When I return to my room tonight I will be arrested—and so I've come to say good-by." Both of us knew we would never meet again.

eighteen

VICHY 1942
RESISTANCE

Aɴᴏᴛʜᴇʀ ᴡᴏʀᴅ ᴘᴇᴄᴜʟɪᴀʀ ᴛᴏ
our situation in the relief work was "T.E.," our contraction
of the French "travailleurs etrangers"—"foreign laborers."
When you were speaking French they were "Tay Ay."

The main body of these groups at first consisted of foreigners who had been enrolled in the French army or other military
formations now formally demobilized but still maintained
under semimilitary discipline. By mid-1942 we began to hear
of additions to these groups formed by the French under
instructions from the Germans.

These formations served a dual purpose: workers were
sorely needed, but the groups also provided a convenient
method for the surveillance of foreigners in France.

The official proclamation authorizing these detachments

stated that able-bodied men between eighteen and fifty-six were to be included. The facts were quite different. Some boys of fifteen were mobilized. Many men belonged to the professional classes and were quite inexperienced in—even physically incapable of—the heavy labor to which they were assigned: road building, logging or mining.

Even more unfortunate was the fact that normal health precautions were not observed. The half dozen Czech miners drafted into coal mines told me they were astounded at the lack of safety precautions and the consequent high accident rate. The same callous attitude prevailed in certain chemical factories, where the fumes soon produced serious skin inflammations. What such an atmosphere did to men's lungs is imaginable; still, no man was released from the chemical works until he began to spit blood. I saw numerous such lung cases in our Château de la Blancherie in Marseilles.

By April, 1942, some forty thousand men were enrolled in the labor gangs. Since they were scattered in small groups, usually away from urban centers in out-of-the-way corners of the country, our committee found it difficult to serve them. Even if travel had been less difficult, we did not have the personnel to spare from service in the refugee camps. However, many of these laborers had come from camps where they had known the service of our various agencies, so we all kept receiving appeals for help.

Material relief was out of the question: it was clearly up to the European Student Relief and the YMCA. After much negotiation with the authorities, the two agencies arranged a circulating library system. From Switzerland we imported hundreds of uniform wooden boxes, each holding about ten pounds of books. When these boxes arrived to start the project, they so crowded our little office in the rue Pythéas that we almost had to move out. Postal service was still functioning, and could reach even the most remote places in southern France, so soon our book boxes were in every work camp. One man in each camp was detailed as correspondent and librarian and once a given shipment of books had been read, it was returned to our office and we forwarded another. Some of the most touching letters I received in Marseilles came from men in these labor battalions, in appreciation of the circulating libraries.

With every month the situation of the T.E. worsened. The Nîmes Commission on the T.E. brought in alarming reports. With typical lack of concern, the police had thrown these groups of foreigners together. A small detachment of twenty men might contain men of five nationalities and languages, and the consequent lack of understanding was anything but favorable to good spirit and good work.

Furthermore, there was the ever-recurring danger that these anti-Nazi foreigners might be turned over to the Germans. The Germans were now pushing France to furnish five hundred thousand "volunteers" for their war industry, and Frenchmen were doing their utmost to avoid being sent. It seemed likely that these foreigners would be offered instead. This threatened possibility soon became fact, and as they began to transport workers to Germany the Nazis divided them into two groups: "Aryan" and "Palestinian."

After consulting the Executive Committee of the Nîmes Committee I invited the Vichy office responsible for the T.E. to send representatives to our next meeting. That was in April, 1942. The meeting turned out to be what the French call "mouvementée." Three men from Vichy turned up: two rather low-brow bandit types and a third really nice gentleman with waxed mustaches, who knew nothing. The delegation at first took the attitude that our committee of some thirty experts in relief work were as ill informed as the third gentleman, but after we had put them through a grueling afternoon they reported to Vichy that they were too exhausted to describe the session.

Nonetheless, during the proceedings we secured promises of reform in some phases of the treatment of foreign workmen and also secured something hitherto unobtainable: general permission for our various organizations to visit the labor camps. It is an interesting detail that all requests for such permits had to have my signature and guarantee, as chairman of the Nîmes Committee. Our committee had become something more important than a simple consultative body of relief workers.

Economic conditions in southern France reached a new low in 1942. In Marseilles the story went round about a local fisherman who caught a specially fine fish and took it home to his wife, where the following conversation ensued: "Just cook this fish in butter, nothing else, it will be fine." "But you must know we have no such thing as butter; it hasn't been seen in this house for a year." "Well, cook it in oil, then." "You must be crazy, there is no more oil than butter." "Well, then just boil it well, it will be good even that way." "But have you forgotten that we have no gas?" Hereupon the man rushed back to the Old Harbor and threw the fish into the sea, where it swam off shouting, "Vive Maréchal Pétain!"

Deficiencies in food and clothing were matched by scarcities in fuel and housing. This was due in large part to increasing German demands, although the Vichy Minister of Agriculture, Bonnafous, announcing new drastic restrictions, complained that "the Anglo-Saxon blockade has greatly impaired France's ability to meet German needs." Early that year there were street demonstrations in three Mediterranean cities because meat, milk and fats had completely disappeared from the public market. Even staples like rice and potatoes had become highly prized rarities. Food ration cards had almost become a joke, since many of the items mentioned simply did not exist.

Results of food shortages were sadly evident among French children. Schools were sending increasing numbers of pupils to clinics for pre-t.b. treatment. In a school canteen run by the Quakers in Marseilles, which provided one extra meal per day, children who went home for Easter vacation were weighed before and after the holidays: without the Quaker food 80 per cent of them lost from one to six pounds during vacation. Black market rates reached catastrophic figures. Oil, normally priced at 12 francs, could be obtained "under the counter" for 150; bread, legally priced at 3.25 fr., cost 50.

Unless they could afford black market prices, foreigners suffered most from the shortages. Most refugees were dependent on the official refugee allowance, and in several southern provinces anything a refugee family might earn was now deducted from the monthly allocation. Shopkeepers naturally would share what supplies they had with their regular clients rather than outsiders. The same situation obtained with regard to clothing. Whatever a family had had at the outset of the war was by now worn out. New materials were almost nonexistent. The official clothing coupons having produced small results, the populace was informed that one new suit (of poorest quality) could be obtained by turning in two old suits. Shoes for adults were equally difficult to come by, and in some parts of France it was now no longer possible to have old shoes repaired, while for children, even at black market prices, shoes were practically unobtainable.

If conditions were hard for Frenchmen, they were doubly so for people in camps. Deaths from starvation were occurring daily, while the total death rate tripled, due in part to the famine, in part to cold, and in part to disease, against which camp populations no longer had any resistance. Our "Nîmes" agencies were straining all reserves to meet the need of hundreds of men and women afflicted with famine dropsy. I shall never forget the picture of starving Jews lined up outside the American Friends Service Center in Rivesaltes, waiting for their daily food supplement. But private initiative was manifestly insufficient, and the hoped-for French government intervention never arrived.

By August Vichy was requiring all vineyard owners to turn in a given quantity of copper, to obtain the copper sulphate essential for spraying their vines, and you would see small piles of old copper pots and discarded rain spouts near the gates of great winegrowers. As if further to outrage Frenchmen, from now on nothing stronger than wine could be sold in restaurants and cafés.

The French people's reaction to Vichy's new restrictions paralleled the restrictions themselves. All over southern France, in the larger cities such as Marseilles and Béziers, there were protest parades on July 14, "Bastille Day," as suggested by de Gaulle's radio from Britain. Some of these demonstrations got out of hand, but the police simply looked the other way. In the Gardanne coal mines someone cut most of the elevator cables.

In an effort to counteract the rising unrest, Vichy now had a staff of two hundred, expressly engaged in an attempt to popularize Marshal Pétain. This department, installed in one of the grand hotels, occupied twelve times the floor space of the Ministry of Foreign Affairs. The idea seemed to be that if the Marshal's portrait and his sayings could be repeated often enough Frenchmen would come to like him. In addition to stamps and coins, the Marshal appeared on milk bottles, telephone poles, all public buildings. Nine biographies of Pétain were published. Not for one minute was a Frenchmen allowed to forget the Chief of State.

The French press gave us practically no news. Earlier, Swiss papers coming into France had provided a certain antidote to the French press. Then it was ordered that anything printed in French in Switzerland for introduction into France must pass French (i.e., German) censorship. This order applied even to such nonpolitical material as the bulletin of the World Council of Churches. Since I was shuttling between France and Switzerland, I could compare the Swiss and French editions of some newspapers. The material was altered to a surprising degree. Everything indicating an Allied success was eliminated, so that an article, quite objective in the Swiss version, appeared in French in a form indicating unbroken triumphs for the Axis powers. Before this censorship was instituted, Swiss papers had been selling in France in several times the numbers of their local Swiss circulation, but as soon as people realized the true state of affairs, the rich profits from sales in France were ended.

One of the attractions advertised to gain volunteers for work in German factories was the promise that for every French volunteer the Nazis would repatriate one French prisoner of war. There was a thin sprinkle of credulous volunteers. By August one Marseilles editor declared that he was weary of announcing that the first train of returned war prisoners would soon arrive, and he would not mention the matter again whether the trainload came or not. Soon it was evident that the small number of war prisoners actually returned were men in the last stage of grave illness, and after that there were no more volunteers.

French resistance was mounting with every passing week. It took various forms, not all of them violent. The Germans took 1,500 new trucks from a French factory and exported them to Tunisia. None of them was ever seen in action, because of sabotage at the factory, and the only indication of their fate was Nazi criticism of German officers for careless inspection before acceptance. One of my friends ran a garage in Marseilles and with each German car he had to repair he made a practice of dropping two cubes of sugar into the gas tank just before the car left. This guaranteed the blocking of the motor after a few miles of driving.

With the evident mission of bringing German culture to the barbarian French, the Nazis arranged a concert in Lyon by the Berlin Philharmonic Orchestra. The Lyon student association bought up all the tickets so that the hall would be quite empty for the concert. However, someone gave the scheme away to the Nazis and that evening a goodly number of police and some German and Italian officers made up the sparse audience. The orchestra played for twenty minutes and then called off the concert.

Edouard Herriot, grand old man, was under house arrest because of his letters of protest to Pétain. Incurring Vichy's

wrath in 1940 by refusing its request for a list of the Jewish
members of Parliament, he had not ceased writing protest
letters.

Archbishop Saliège of Toulouse issued a personal letter to
be read "without comment" in all churches. Since Laval had
forbidden all publicity about the deportations, now becoming
a matter of common knowledge, the Archbishop was making
the protest his personal responsibility. "There is," he wrote,
"a Christian decency and a human morality that impose
duties and confer rights. These derive from the very nature
of man. They may be violated, but no mortal has the power
to suppress them. That children, women and men, fathers
and mothers, should be treated like a wretched herd, that
members of the same family should be separated and embarked
for an unknown destination, was a sad spectacle reserved for
our times to witness. The Jews are our brethren. They belong
to mankind. No Christian dare forget that. Why does the
right of asylum no longer exist in our country? Why are we
a vanquished people? Lord have mercy upon us."

Other leaders were more definite. Cardinal Gerlier refused
Vichy's request that he instruct Catholics who were hiding
Jewish children to surrender them to the police. General de
Saint-Vincent, military governor of Lyon, was dismissed by
Laval because he refused to place his troops at the disposal
of the government so that they could make mass arrests of
Jews. All over southern France Christian families and institu-
tions had begun hiding Jewish families or individuals.

One day in Rivesaltes I discovered five Jewish children
from our Czech colony in Vence, all marked for deportation.
The fact that we had our representatives resident in this camp
made it possible to secure the release of three children by
more or less legal methods, and although their parents were
with them awaiting certain deportation, we managed to get
the other two out of camp, hidden in a delivery truck. All
five went into hiding and lived until the war was over.

A lighter side of the tragic situation was a violent epidemic of marriages all over southern France. In the early weeks of deportations, Jews married to Christians were exempted from seizure. Later the rule was changed, and the Christian member of the couple had to choose between being left alone or accompanying the husband or wife. But at first all sorts of matches, some contemplated for years and others concocted under pressure of the emergency, were arranged. A pastor I know received this telegram from a Jewish member of a foreign labor gang which, the previous year, had been quartered in his town: "Will marry immediately any girl in your parish, preferably Louise."

To all our rescue efforts the Germans reacted by imposing even stricter controls. Under Vichy orders the police checkpoint at Annemasse, the one "open" railroad station between France and Switzerland, was reinforced. Police began arresting Frenchmen known to be "passers" over the line into Switzerland. Despite these precautions, by the end of October, 1942, six thousand refugees had crossed into Swiss territory and about a thousand had gone over the Spanish frontier. The Swiss government set up a special commissariat to deal with the increasing problem of refugees. Within ten days during October more than two thousand persons had crossed the Swiss frontier illegally. If they could not pay large sums to boatmen to row them across Lake Geneva, the only other possible route was the tortuous and difficult climb over the already snow-clad mountains, hiding by day and going on by night. Out of one group that had arrived in Geneva one day when I was there, fifteen persons at the start, two had died en route and two others had feet so badly frozen that amputation was necessary.

In France mass arrests continued throughout September; hundreds of persons were seized daily and sent to Rivesaltes. That enormous camp in southwest France was, from then on, to be the sifting place for all the Jews rounded up by the police. Inside this camp was the sorting pen—a large barbedwire enclosure into which all those arrested were put until the sifting commission could examine their cases and decide whether or not they were to be deported. If sheep were sufficiently intelligent, it would not be difficult to imagine their mental anguish as the butchers looked over a flock to see which they would choose for slaughter. Such was the atmosphere of this prison within a prison. One of the most ghastly aspects was that many of these poor people had been through the sorting process two or three times already and were still waiting for another trial. They had seen the trucks roll out of their prison with people being turned over to the Germans, themselves saved from this transport but possible members of the next. One fine woman who had passed twice before the sorting commission and been held for further investigation said to me: "Mr. Lowrie, there are just no words for it."

The October session of the Nîmes Committee met under the shadow of these terrible events. It opened with a moving statement by the Grand Rabbi of France, expressing gratitude for the sympathy and helpfulness of our organizations. We made plans for the immediate future and linked our efforts even more closely. Again, as throughout these tragic years, mutual confidence between Christians and Jews was manifested. In one camp where Christians were permitted to attend church services in the town, the YMCA club was turned into a synagogue once a week. In most camps all religious services had to be held in our "foyers," but great care was taken in decoration and design to avoid using any symbolism that might offend our Jewish friends. I noted this concern in a letter: "Everywhere the Christian forces, Catholic and Protestant, have been not only serving Jews in distress to the measure of their ability, but have stood, and are standing, heroically to their defense. And the absolute confidence with which our Jewish friends ask and accept such help is another sign of a relationship almost unprecedented in our day." One day the head of a Jewish organization came to see me. "I have several hundred young people in my group," he said, "what are you going to do about helping to hide them from the police?" In view of the prevailing relationship, this was a very natural question. And of course something was done about it. Not since the times of religious persecution had there been so many people in France hiding others from the arm of the law. What with procuring false passports, smuggling people across boundaries, and helping others avoid police searches, I wondered if most of us would ever become law-abiding citizens again.

Thanks to the considerate help of the Bishop of Tulle, nearest city to our Czech farms, nine of our Jewish farmers were saved from deportation. The farm manager called on the Bishop and explained that we had men on the farms who were "orthodox," and since the police did not seem to know that the Orthodox Church was a good Christian religion, along with Catholic and Protestant churches, would the Bishop give a certificate that it was? Fully conscious of the actual situation, His Grace wrote each of the men concerned a personal letter: "Dear Mr. Silberstein: In response to your inquiry, I am pleased to inform you that the Eastern Orthodox Church is one of the world's universally recognized Christian churches," and he affixed his "tremendous" episcopal seal. The police were so surprised that Silberstein had a "certificate" from the Bishop that they accepted the letter for the impression it was intended to convey, and so nine more men escaped deportation trains.

In Lyon one day the police arrived at the gates of a convent, demanding entrance to search for Jewish children reportedly hidden there. The Mother Superior replied that if the policemen did not remove themselves from her doorstep instantly she would telephone the Cardinal, and then gave them such a lecture on the inviolability of a convent that they never came back.

One amusing instance of Christian-Jewish cooperation occurred when HICEM, the ancient and honorable Hebrew Emigration Society, asked the Czech Aid for the privilege of arranging the emigration of some Christians. They explained that this would prove to Vichy authorities that HICEM was an organization making no racial distinctions.

The Spanish frontier guards might accept such refugees, but this passage practically assured a month at least in Spanish prisons. One day one of our Czech staff was escorting a group of eight across the Pyrenees frontier. "We are just going over to the fiesta in that village," he told the Spanish guard. "All right," the guard replied; "when you come back you might bring me a bottle of cognac." When, a few hours later, the young man not only returned but also brought the cognac, the guard could scarcely believe his senses.

While thousands were escaping from unoccupied France, others were escaping into it from the north. All sorts of devices were used. One of our Czechs walked from Paris across the whole of German-occupied France and over the line, carrying a halter and looking for "a gray horse that strayed out this way."

During those hectic weeks it seemed that most of my time was spent in travel. A few lines from a letter of that time record a typical week: "Thursday noon I was in the plane for Vichy . . . Six hours in Vichy—time for four appointments, and I took the train for Toulouse, a twelve-hour trip. This train carries no sleeper . . . I had seven hours in Toulouse, and then went on to Pau."

During these months it was necessary to visit Geneva about once every ten days in order to communicate with New York and maintain contact with representatives of a half dozen governments. Crossing the frontier was always an interesting experience. Behind each uniformed customs officer stood a man in civilian clothes: a German surveying the border. Annemasse was the one legally open crossing point between "free France" and Switzerland. As an American citizen whose government maintained friendly relations with both these states, I had the right to move between them at will.

The Germans would make a wry face as they looked at my

passport, and on several occasions would tell the Frenchman: "Take him in and search him." So the customs officer and I would retire to one of the little booths provided for the purpose, but never once was I searched.

The Frenchman would say: "You must know how I dislike this, but you know how things are—let's have a cigarette." After a proper interval we would emerge, my passport would be stamped, and I could board my train for Geneva.

Even if they had searched me they would, of course, have found nothing illegal. Often I was carrying important information to be shared with American officials in Switzerland, but I carried it in my head, and here, as long as the Germans held strictly to legality, they would never know what I was transporting.

nineteen

CHAMBON-SUR-LIGNON

IN SOME SECTIONS OF FRANCE A village is either wholly Protestant or wholly Catholic. This distinction prevails in most cities as well: if you are a Protestant, you trade usually with Protestant shopkeepers, or the reverse if you are Catholic. One of the best-known Protestant villages in southern France is Chambon-sur-Lignon, in the hills above Lyon. The most important institution in the town is the Collège Cévenol, a top-grade preparatory school. And both school and town have always accepted the leadership of the local Protestant clergy, who are also part of the college teaching staff.

Chambon was already well acquainted with refugees before the Jews began to come. When the remnants of republican armies in Spain began to pour over the border into France,

two years before the 1940 debacle, they were apportioned out
to different parts of the country, and Chambon welcomed its
share. The Spanish refugee families made themselves useful
in the town, and left their monument there, in one of the
best-built camps the French YMCA possesses, constructed
by these unwilling guests from Spain.

Then, at the outset of war, thousands of families were
evacuated from frontier sections of Alsace. Every southern
French town had to take in its quota of these homeless people
and find the necessary housing. The resultant clash between
French citizens of German background and citizens in small
French villages who had never been outside their own com-
munities, produced many problems for social work agencies.
Chambon accepted its portion of Alsatians, most of them
Protestant, which made adjustment easier.

When the deportations began, besides several children's
homes there were three centers for refugees in Chambon,
managed by three of the different organizations belonging
to our Coordination Committee. Among the residents in these
homes, the majority of them people liberated from internment
camps, there were over a hundred Jews.

Most French Protestants have never ceased protesting since
Huguenot days. Chambon was outraged by the reports of
Jewish arrests and deportations. Almost as if it had been
planned, Vichy soon gave the townspeople a chance to register
their opinions.

Late in the summer of 1942 the Vichy Minister for Youth,
Lamirand, making a propaganda tour of the region, came to
Chambon accompanied by the Préfet and called a meeting
of youth organizations. His speech extolling Marshal Pétain
was received politely, but afterward a delegation of thirty
senior students at the college, with their two pastors, waited
on him to present their formal protest against what Vichy
was doing with the Jews. "And we must tell you, Monsieur
le Préfet," they said, "that if any attempt is made to molest
the Jewish guests in our village, we will resist, and our

teachers too."

This was something new in the préfet's experience. He spluttered that the deportations were not anti-Semitic "persecution" but simply a regrouping of European Jews in Poland. Then he inadvertently admitted that he had received Vichy orders to take the Jews from Chambon. Growing more angry and red-faced with every minute, he turned on the two pastors: "Be careful! I know what you've been doing here. I can show you letters I've received. When the time comes, we'll get your Jews, and you'd better let them go peaceably." And he stalked out of the room.

That same week the pastors and their students made plans to hide their Jewish guests. If refugees were not a novelty in Chambon history, neither was their concealment. Some of the hideouts chosen had been used three hundred years before by the Huguenots. The whole countryside was alerted, and scarcely a farmer refused to take in a refugee should this become necessary.

On a Saturday afternoon a fortnight after the first visit the police came again, this time with two large khaki-colored buses which drew up in the village square. The police captain called on Pastor M. in his study: "We know you know all the Jews in this town—give us a list."

"But of course you don't really expect me to do that," the pastor replied. "Would you, in my place?"

"Well, then, you can at least sign this," and the captain held out an official poster: "Appeal to Jews." The notice urged all Jews in Chambon to turn themselves in to the police, quietly. This would avoid all risk to families which had been sheltering Jews and prevent any disturbance of public order. By this time the other Chambon pastor had joined Pastor M. "But we cannot sign this," they assured the gendarme.

The police captain wasted no more words. "You'll sign it by tomorrow noon or I'll arrest both of you." "Tomorrow noon," he growled, as he slammed the door behind him.

That night was a busy one for Chambon. Something went wrong with the town's lighting system, but darkness seemed not to hinder considerable movement. The police, waiting for their ultimatum to expire, slept in their buses. The Sunday morning church service was tense and the pastors expected to find the police waiting to arrest them as they went out into the street.

Instead, the gendarmes had begun their house-to-house search. Every house in the village, as well as most of the nearby farms, was rigorously inspected from cellar to attic. They found one Jew who had not hidden because half his ancestors had been Aryan. Villagers could scarcely keep from smiling as they passed those twenty gendarmes sitting in their two buses with their one captive. Someone brought the prisoner a homemade cake. Others quickly took the hint, and before long the meek-looking little man had a heap of presents that filled more space in the bus than he did. This was one way of showing complete solidarity with the pastors.

On Monday morning the shamefaced police had to release their sole captive, who had presented documentary proof that he was half "Aryan." However, they began a new combing-over of the town and the country around it that continued, on and off, for more than a fortnight. Although twenty gendarmes hunted the woods and made countless surprise house searches in the town, not a single arrest could be made, and at last they departed in their two army buses.

I said not one person had been arrested in Chambon, but there was one exception which proved very interesting. Madame Durand (that is not her name), "grande dame" of the village, had taken one of the Jewish refugees, a girl student, into her home. When first she heard of impending police action, Madame Durand went to the commissaire of police at once. "I give notice," she said, "that I have a girl named Greta at my house and I assume complete responsibility for her." That was that, and Madame Durand and the entire family went peacefully to bed. At three in the morning the police took the girl, despite Madame Durand's outraged protests. At six o'clock Madame Durand was in the train for Vichy. Before the day was over she had interviewed the Minister of Foreign Affairs and the Chief of Police, a man almost as hard to see as the Pope. In the meantime the girl had been put into a train and was on her way to Germany. Fortunately she was taken out of the car before it crossed the demarcation line, and so was saved, at least for this time. From then on Madame Durand addressed reams of letters to all her friends telling of the terrible thing that had happened to her. As propaganda for further resistance the incident was most fortunate.

"La Maison des Roches," the European Student Relief home for refugees in Chambon, experienced particularly dramatic episodes. Its residents were all university students who had been released from various internment camps through the efforts of the Nîmes Committee. The students were of nine different nationalities: ten of them were Aryan, twenty-one were Jewish. Here in the Collège Cévenol these young men could continue their studies. To help them with the French language, four French students from the Collège came to live with them in La Maison des Roches.

After German occupation of southern France, the residents of La Maison des Roches, like the rest of the people of Chambon, lived in a state of constant alert. Time and again there would be a rumor that the Gestapo were about to search the house, and there would be a general exodus to the woods. Since most of the police raids seemed to take place at night, students would sleep in the woods and come back to the house by day. A red-checkered towel hung in a certain window informed them that the coast was clear.

This uncertainty so disrupted any orderly study that the young French director of the house made a special trip to Vichy to explore the atmosphere there. To his discreet inquiries the authorities gave assurance that no arrests in his house were contemplated. This assurance turned out to be as good as most of Laval's promises, and within a fortnight, possibly because the director's Vichy inquiry had called attention to Les Roches, the house was suddenly visited one summer morning by the dreaded Gestapo, demanding entrance. The courageous young director stalled with them at the front entrance, while all the Jewish students escaped by a rear door.

Of course the whole village was concerned about what might be happening in the student home, but how could anyone manage to pass the police cordon? A retired clergyman finally hit upon a scheme. He told the Gestapo men he was afraid something might happen to a valuable book he had lent one of the students, and so was permitted to enter the house. He returned to tell the townsfolk that Les Roches was in terror. The police were using their customary method of questioning plus physical coercion. It looked as though the whole group of students, all refugees but none of them Jews, would be carried away, and apparently nothing could be done to save them.

Here a pastor's wife intervened. She knew that one of the Austrian students at Les Roches had saved the life of a German soldier who had been stricken with cramps while swimming in the little river and who would have drowned without the young Austrian's timely help. As the pastor's wife she could and did call at the local German army headquarters, demanding to see the officer in charge. "Would you let that student who risked his life to save one of your men be arrested by the Gestapo?" she asked him. When he said no, the pastor's wife insisted that he accompany her to Les Roches and tell the story. Now, no minor officer would ever of his own accord cross swords with the all-powerful Gestapo, but such was the lady's persistence that this one reluctantly went with her. She managed to pass the police line by saying she was the cleaning woman, come as usual for her work. Inside, she put on a blue apron and took over in the kitchen, serving coffee to the Gestapo inquisitors. Once in their presence, she

was able to insist that the German officer tell the story of the
Austrian student and the rescue. As a result, he was the only
man of the residents to escape deportation. The Gestapo,
realizing how they had been tricked by the director at the
entrance, took him away with the other students and for
good measure the four French students also. The young
director never returned.

Neither did most of the other Aryans. The case of one of the
four French students was particularly distressing. Of Jewish
origin, he was himself a Christian. Foreseeing possible interro-
gation, he had once asked his pastor what he should say about
himself under questioning. The pastor had said that he need
not mention his Jewish parents: he should simply insist that
he was a Christian, his French nationality and his membership
in the Christian church should assure his safety. . . . The
Gestapo in Chambon did not discover the young man's racial
ancestry, but once he was in a concentration camp in Germany—with full knowledge of what was happening to Jews
all around him—his conscience so plagued him that he went
to the commandant and revealed his Jewish parentage. He
was immediately shipped out of that camp and was never
heard from again.

The day Les Roches was raided the two pastors also were
arrested and interned in Gurs. However, powerful intervention
secured their release within two months, and they could
continue as the center of activity in Chambon.

If the local Chambon police had ever sympathized with
Vichy's plan to eliminate the Jews, German occupation
certainly changed their minds. The long-drawn-out anguish
of hiding hundreds of Jews for months on end could never
have been as successful as it was without the secret collaboration of friends in the local police office. Before almost every
raid word would be passed around indicating what houses
were to be searched. Somehow this system failed in the case
of Les Roches.

Chambon was an outstanding example of the feeling that had

developed across the whole of France. Everywhere Christian
people were helping Jews to escape the Nazi clutches. One
man I knew lived for weeks with four other refugees in a
cellar whose entrance was concealed under a trash pile.
Another walked for six days along the railroad track posing
as a workman, tapping the switches with his hammer, often
passing police checkpoints undetected. A fascinating story
could be written about disguises and subterfuges that helped
Jewish refugees to elude their pursuers. Near Marseilles the
children held in a detention camp learned that the age limit
for exemption from deportation had been lowered from
eighteen to sixteen, whereupon the fourteen boys between
those two ages left for the woods before the police should
come to get them. They were adopted by a troop of French
Boy Scouts, and for weeks lived in the woods like Indians,
fed secretly by their Scout protectors. In Chambon one day
a large group of children from the Swiss Aid home got through
the police cordon thrown around the village by donning
Scout uniforms and marching out, singing French Scouting
songs they had been practicing for weeks for just such an
emergency. Scores of Jews, particularly children, found escape from the Chambon area impossible and never left it until
the end of the war.

To their indiscretions in hiding Jews, the people of Chambon
added the crime of helping the Resistance. Chambon became
a minor headquarters for the "Maquis," the secret Resistance
army, and the symbiosis of these two groups, the one led by
the pastors refusing, as a matter of principle, the use of
violence and the other existing principally to employ force
against the Germans, was one of the exciting experiences of
those years. Each group respected the other, each trusted the
other's devotion to the same cause. Finally, as one of the
pastors later told me, they could scarcely decide which group
did more to protect the other. It was a double spy of the
Maquis—a man the Nazis employed for espionage who was
secretly reporting to the French—who warned the Chambon

pastors so that they were able to go into hiding just before
the Gestapo came a second time to seize them.

When, a little later, the American OSS began dropping
parachutists into southern France the Chambon churchyard
was a favorite target. One American who broke a leg in the
operation was cared for in the local hospital until he was able
to travel, although the Germans, now in full control, made
frequent visits in the town looking for suspicious characters.

By the time the Germans occupied all of France the fame
of Chambon had spread far and wide. The whole countryside
became one vast clandestine organization, with practically
every farm sheltering a Jewish family. After the war, Jewish
relief agencies estimated that more than a thousand different
Jews had spent some time in this brave and hospitable community. To the Jews the word Chambon meant helpfulness;
to the police, and particularly to the Gestapo who came in
with the Nazi army, the name was odious. Time and again
they struck at this hated symbol of resistance.

One day the pastor was being questioned by the Gestapo
about his activities in caring for Jews. He told them that it
was his duty as a Christian, adding that he would do the same
for Germans should the occasion arise. It did: at the end of
the war a large war-prisoner camp was established just outside
Chambon, and in the face of somewhat violent criticism by
local citizenry the pastor began at once to minister to the
Germans there.

twenty

DESTINATION UNKNOWN

O N AUGUST 13 (1942) WE SENT
this cable to the JDC headquarters in New York: "3,600 Jews
from internment camps in unoccupied France sent eastward,
exact destination unknown, 1,000 from Gurs, 1,000 from
Rivesaltes, 700 Vernet. Mass arrests made in hotels Bompard
and Levante, Marseilles. 200 women taken to Les Milles for
deportation. Order affects men and women aged 18–65.
Mothers have choice of taking with them children over five
or leaving them with welfare organizations. Total quota is
10,000, first from camps, then working groups. If quota not
attained, then arrests to be made in cities."

Ten days earlier, what we had been fearing for months had
eventuated. We all knew that the Germans had been moving
thousands of Jews eastward from occupied France to un-

known destinations, but this was the first time the Nazis had
struck into what both they and Marshal Pétain still called
Free France. Despite the velvet assurances of Laval or
Darquier de Pellepoix, General Commissioner for Jewish
Affairs, that no violence would be applied to Jews in southern
France, the last word evidently belonged to Hitler's prime
Jew hater, Rosenberg. *Paris Soir* explained that four thousand
Jews from occupied territory and an equal number from
unoccupied France had been deported eastward, "as a lesson
to the Jewish accomplices of terrorists and black marketeers."

In Marseilles the shock of those August hotel raids struck
us all with peculiar force. The two modest hotels mentioned
in our cable were occupied largely by refugees, mostly Jews,
who happened to have sufficient means to avoid internment
in a camp. The poor people were routed from their beds at
four in the morning, given just time to dress, advised to take
a blanket and supplies for a day's journey. Loaded into trucks,
they were taken to the railroad station, packed into boxcars
and transported to Les Milles.

What happened there brought terror and suffering almost
unimaginable. One of the special police at Les Milles later
told me he had lived in the colonies and China, had fought in
two wars, but never had witnessed such scenes. It began with
the arrival of fully armed national police who surrounded
the camp, refusing entrance to all outsiders. For several days
even chaplains, Christian and Jewish, were denied admission.
The camp officials were working day and night making and
remaking lists for deportation. No one knew who would be
taken and what chance a given person had of escaping the
general fate.

A few days later the actual choice of victims began. By
this time pastors and rabbis had forced the authorities to admit
them to the camps and they joined our workers in a veritable
battle for rescue. In most places the local Catholic priests felt
they could not intervene without special hierarchical permission, and this could not be obtained in time.

The day after the first mass arrests in Marseilles I chaired an emergency committee composed of representatives of the Friends Service Committee, the International Migration Service, the Swiss Aid, the OSE, the International Rescue Union, the YMCA and the YWCA, to face the new terror and decide what we could do, as individual organizations or acting together. It was little enough, Heaven knows. First there were protests, to Vichy and then to the world. We alerted all the news agencies, we sent cables to all governments still maintaining relations with the Pétain regime. We heard reports that Pope Pius had protested to Pétain and that Laval had agreed "for the moment" to limit deportations to foreign Jews.

However exact this report, leading clergy in France did protest in no uncertain terms. The brave Archbishop Saliège of Toulouse protested from the pulpit: "Jewish children, men and women are being treated like cattle." Dr. Marc Boegner, President of the Protestant Federation of France, the country's leading Protestant, consulted with Cardinal Gerlier and they each wrote Pétain a letter of the same content. "No Frenchman," wrote Boegner, "can remain insensible to what has happened in the internment camps since August second. . . . There are about to be delivered to Germany men and women who from political or religious motives have sought refuge in France. . . . The Christian churches, of whatever faith, would be unfaithful to their duty if they did not raise a protest." In allusion to Pétain's frequent insistence that France was a defeated nation, Boegner continued: "I beseech you to impose the measures indispensable if France is not to inflict upon itself a moral defeat, the burden of which would be incalculable."

Our Nîmes emergency committee alerted all the other members, asking them to address protests to governments, Red Cross societies, and newspapers. But these moves could not save the first convoy from deportation. We decided to appeal to Marshal Pétain himself. Two of us, president and vice-president of the Nîmes Committee, went at once to Vichy.

Mobilizing all the pressures available from sympathetic French notables and the United States Embassy—who could intervene directly in Pétain's "cabinet"—and from newspapermen and others who could approach the Foreign Office, we demanded an audience with the Chief of the French State.

Our first contact was with Pétain's personal secretary, General Campet. This gentleman had never heard of the deportations. Further, he assured us that such a thing would not be possible in France. If we had not insisted upon seeing him, it is probable that Pétain would have heard of these atrocities only later, if at all. After we had spent three days canvassing various agencies we were informed that the head of the French State would receive us in audience. This was two days before the first deportation train was scheduled to leave.

One of Vichy's swank hotels was now in effect the capital of France, since it housed the executive offices of the Chief of State. Passing the tired-looking soldiers on guard at the entrance, we waited only a few minutes in an anteroom, then we were shown into an office rather crowded with furniture, desks and tables covered with a large amount of bric-à-brac. The working desk itself seemed orderly.

We were presented by the Marshal's General Secretary, M. Jardelle, and were seated in two chairs facing the Marshal with Jardelle at his side, but between us and Pétain. Before Pétain could reply to anything we said, Jardelle restated it to him in his own words in a slightly louder voice, thus suggesting the reply. Before the interview we had presented a formal memo stating that we represented all the private philanthropic organizations in France, that we were spending 80 per cent of our budgets for the aid of French people, and consequently only a minor part of our work was for refugees. The Marshal had supposedly been informed of this memo. Pétain asked, "What gives me the honor of your visit?"

"We come to you in the name of all the philanthropic organizations in France working in large part for the French population, but also for foreign refugees. Many of our organizations have given major aid to the French," I replied. Here Jardelle interrupted to name the Quakers and the YMCA.

"I know both of these and we are grateful for their help," the Marshal said.

I went on: "For two years these organizations have been collaborating with the French government, often at the government's request, to help preserve and prepare these refugees for emigration. About 10,000 have already emigrated, thanks to our combined efforts. We are willing to continue this service, but we are now greatly concerned about the present measures being taken against certain foreign refugees, particularly Spanish and Jews."

Jardelle, interrupting, "You know, Monsieur le Maréchal, that the Germans asked to have 10,000 French Jews and that to save them we have been obliged to give up an equal number of foreign Jews. They are to be transported to a sort of 'Jewish state' the Germans have set up near Lublin. There, it appears, they will enjoy a certain liberty."

"Oh, yes, I know, near Krakow," said Pétain. (The old man was wrong—he meant Kattowitz.)

"We have been deeply moved and profoundly hurt by the present measures," I continued. "We cannot believe, Monsieur le Maréchal, that this has been done with your knowledge [this I emphasized, but Pétain did not react] or that it is inevitable."

Pétain made a gesture of helplessness, open hands and a shrug of his shoulders. "You know our situation with regard to the Germans."

Of course we could not accept this as an answer. I took the approach we had previously discussed in committee: "We believe that there might at least be some exemptions. For example, those ready to emigrate. Laval has this list under study." Here both Pétain and Jardelle brightened and Pétain said he would speak to Laval about it. I went on: "Then, the children. We can naturally make no promises but we believe

that if we could have three or four weeks in which to launch
an appeal United States doors might be open for the children
involved."

"I will speak of this to Laval, too. Will you be in Vichy for
a week or ten days to have a reply?"

"Monsieur le Maréchal, the first train is leaving today."

"Well, then I will speak to Laval this afternoon and you
may telephone M. Jardelle tomorrow for the decision," said
Pétain, and half rose from his chair.

I had to play one more card: "We cannot conceal from you,
Monsieur le Maréchal, the unfortunate impression this action
will have on public opinion abroad and the serious repercus-
sions it may have on the work of our organizations in France."

Pétain simply waved his hand as though he deprecated this,
and then rose, terminating the interview. We had the impression that he had not fully grasped the last remark.

Pétain was not as tall as his pictures had led us to believe.
He held himself erect and had a fairly firm handclasp.
Although he seemed physically well preserved, his flesh was
bloodless, almost waxen in color. He was slightly deaf and
evidently not altogether aware of what went on around him.

While I was appealing to Pétain, Quaker representatives,
acting on behalf of the Nîmes Committee also, saw Laval.
The total result was nil. The old Marshal could do nothing,
Laval would not. His tirade against Jews in general gave every
indication that he approved the atrocious measures. All that
was left for us to do was to fight things out on the local level.

During those hectic days the camp director's office at Les
Milles was like a courtroom gone frantic. The little room was
crowded, coatless men sweated in the August heat, police
inspectors came and went, camp clerks brought in new tele-
grams from Vichy and protests from all sorts of Frenchmen.
There was constant movement, fearful tension. In principle
the director himself, never noted for his love for his charges
but nevertheless a man with some sense of justice, had to make
all decisions. But behind his chair stood a police captain

representing Vichy and, indirectly, Rosenberg and Hitler.

The "attorneys for the defense" were men from our various agencies, an American or two, but most of them French since this was a French problem and Frenchmen were in a better position to argue or insist. Among these none was more effective than Monsieur F., the local pastor. Living near the camp, he knew intimately all its internal life, including the actions and omissions of the management. Like the rest of us, he took the position that no Christian or even a Jew with a Christian spouse could be brought under the deportation order. Each time a list was made up the pastor and others began a new attack on the director. "You know, monsieur, that Morgenstern has been one of the most faithful members in our church." "Yes, but before he came to Les Milles? Some have become Christians overnight." "But here is his baptismal certificate dated 1925—surely he should not be in this new list. Remember his service in our library all these months." —"And here is Rubinstein. You know as well as I that Mrs. Rubinstein is Aryan, and that he became a Christian at the time of their marriage." "We're not taking Madame Rubinstein—" "But how can you face separating this Christian, I repeat, this Christian couple? Put yourself in Rubinstein's place. It is unthinkable that—" In his earnestness the pastor could not keep his voice from betraying his feeling toward the police. "What do you think?" The director turned to the Vichy agent. "Oh, let him stay—at least for this time"—and the director initialed an order releasing Rubinstein from Ilot K.

In the vast confusion no one seemed sure who had authority to grant exemptions—the camp officials, the police, the prefecture, or Vichy. In one case a whole group of politically endangered men who had been exempted by the French authorities were replaced in the deportation lists after a German officer had visited the camp. One was a former captain of a German ship who had served the Allies during World War I. His father and two brothers had been executed in Germany as enemies of the Third Reich. All efforts to save him failed and he left with the first train, calm and courageous in his Christian faith.

Another man was a distinguished lawyer condemned to death in Germany for his activity during the early anti-Nazi trials. He and his wife had been among the mainstays of the Protestant group at Les Milles. Their son was in the Foreign Legion in Africa and this should have assured their exemption. Had they any proof? Thinking to save their son from possible difficulties, they had burned all their papers. A frantic search revealed a letter proving that the son was in the Legion. The authorities replied, "This indicates his presence in the Legion last March—it does not prove he is still there in August." The couple climb calmly into the boxcar and the iron bar falls across the closed door. Some hours later, just before the train moves out, new insistence by the local pastor forces the police to relent, and the two are saved.

Here was a mother, returned voluntarily to the camp from free residence outside to share the fate of her son. The young man, not knowing of her intention and warned of his own danger by a guard, had fled the camp shortly before his mother's arrival. In spite of all efforts by Pastor F. and a YMCA secretary, the mother was sent to the deportation pen.

There was a young man of thirty-six who had come down from the occupied zone to join his wife and children after a long separation. Of Polish origin, he had lived in France since he was a year old. He had volunteered in the French army at the outbreak of the war. He had excellent recommendations from well-known Frenchmen. But he was a Jew. Jewish by race and by religion, as he repeated with magnificent obstinacy each time the question came up. The police had picked him up at a railroad station just before his train was to leave for the village where his family was awaiting him. He could not understand why he had been arrested and brought to Les Milles, and when he was put into the deportation train he kept insisting that he must be permitted to see his wife and children.

In the confusion much unnecessary suffering ensued. French organization, none too strong at best, almost broke down. Men and women were herded into the courtyards and forced to stand for hours under a blazing sun while the final lists were being made. Is it any wonder that in each camp there were suicides?

The actual deportation, unfortunately only the first of a series, was as bad as could be imagined: men and women pushed like cattle into boxcars, thirty to a car with a police guard. The cars' only equipment was a bit of straw on the floor, and one iron pail for all toilet purposes. The journey, we were told, would take a fortnight or eighteen days. The various relief organizations gave what could be obtained in this half-starved land in the way of extra provisions for the journey. The YMCA despairingly put a box of books into each car. All of us were curtly refused permission to accompany the trains or even to organize a service of hot drinks and refreshments at the frontier where the trains would pass into German-occupied territory.

The dignity and self-control of most of these unfortunate people will always be remembered, together with the self-forgetfulness and generosity manifested in such large measure. In many cases internees offered to go in place of others. There were two sisters at Gurs, both over eighty, who went to the director of the camp saying they understood that volunteers would be accepted to replace others on the lists and offering themselves for this purpose. The communion in suffering between Jews and Christians seemed more intimate here than ever—the close collaboration of pastors and rabbis, the unfailing aid offered by Christian organizations, and the confidence with which Jewish groups asked for and accepted it.

There were moments of tragicomedy. Before one deportation (September 26–27) the camp officials worked most of the night, this time out of doors because it was cooler. Two women, picked up on the streets of Toulon, kept running up to Pastor F., who was checking lists at a lamplit table, asking hysterical questions and thus calling police attention to themselves. The pastor finally urged them to remain out of sight. Later the camp secretary shouted their names from his list. No one appeared, but a voice out of the darkness replied: "The pastor told us to hide and not to answer when we were called."

By 3:30 A.M. all those standing in the sorting pen had been checked, and put into the train. The rest, including camp officials, went to bed. At seven the police chief arrived from Marseilles, counted the names of those in the train and found the number short of the quota for this convoy. He ordered people to be taken from the infirmary to make up the total. Men and women in their nightclothes were hustled into the train just before it pulled out.

Alerted because of the new crises, Pastor F. arrived a few minutes before the train left. When he learned that five Jewish Christians had been added to the lists after his departure three hours earlier, he protested vigorously to the police, but in vain. The train was already moving when he located the five in one of the cars. "Don't despair," he called to them, "we're still fighting. Watch out at Lyon." Pastor F. telephoned me in Marseilles and I sent a hot telegram to Vichy. At Lyon the police removed the five men from the train and sent them to temporary safety in Rivesaltes.

Although most of the able-bodied men had already been impressed into the foreign labor battalions, the first group deported consisted of men only. They were told they were being assembled for another work party, which was probably one reason for the docility with which they allowed themselves to be packed into boxcars for the long journey. Another reason, besides the fact that half-starved men were facing heavily armed police, was the naïve assumption, particularly among the German Jews, that law and order would prevail, and that after all even the Nazis would contain themselves within the basic laws with which these people had grown up. For example, there was one old man from Mannheim who had been living on his pension as a German ex-civil servant, who never could understand why he was no longer receiving his monthly allowance: he had written home that he was now living in Gurs—why didn't they send him his pension?

By this time we all knew, and most of the Jews in southern France also knew, of the deportation trains from occupied France to Poland. And frightful rumors had spread regarding the fate of the deportees, but even so, neither in the first instance of deportation from Les Milles nor in any of the others was there any observable effort at resistance. Burdened with almost endless tribulation, these men were as sheep before the slaughter. They conquered hatred by enduring it.

This nonresistance to evil is partly explained as in accord with ancient Hebrew tradition. No small proportion of those who perished in Nazi extermination camps were men of deep religious conviction, and their consent to drink the cup of misery to the last drop, to suffer for their faith, was part and parcel of their spiritual heritage. As the "Nîmes" pastor said, "All have suffered with dignity, with humility and with true greatness."

Just after the first large convoy of Jews had left Les Milles, the director of that camp telephoned, saying he must see me at once. I had known this man about as well as the other camp directors, and thought him like most of the rest: not big enough to resist the super-temptations inherent in his position. There had been ugly tales of near-starvation in his camp while truckloads of provisions went out of it by night, to be sold in the black market of a nearby city. His exploitation of men in his camp for labor in an enterprise from which he drew profits was a matter of open record. A few weeks earlier he had been arrested for profiteering in falsified certificates of liberation.

And he knew that I knew all this, which fact, however, had not affected the surface cordiality of our relationship. I knew of the panic and terror abroad in Les Milles as men were being processed for that week's deportation. So I was not surprised by the director's telephone call. It was midnight when he arrived at our hotel and I could scarcely recognize the man. He had visibly lost weight, his eyes were like those of a hunted animal.

"I never thought I should live through scenes like those in our camp these days," he said. "Having responsibility, even purely executive, for a crime like this is heartrending. I would have resigned at once, but of course it takes time to be relieved of such a position, so I have had to stay and try to make it as easy as possible for those poor people. I have managed to save some of them—the pure Aryans or the half-Aryans I haven't put into the lists, and those with visas for emigration I think we can save also. But artists like B. and musicians like K., men I have the highest admiration for—to send them off to Poland or God knows where, is something so terrible . . .

"I have one request of you, Mr. Lowrie. You know me and you know what is happening now and who is really responsible. Promise me that when the accounts are settled in the future (for there will be a future and there will be a settling of scores, of that I am sure), promise me that you will stand by me and say that this was no responsibility of mine. I am merely carrying out orders—and you know it and you must promise to protect me when vengeance begins."

I never visited Les Milles after the liberation and never heard what became of its director. In the confused and radical adjustments after the war, small attention could be spared for former directors of former refugee-camps, so it is probable that this man moved quietly into some other job.

For weeks we lived in a nightmare, battling with every means at our disposal, legal or not, to save as many as possible from Nazi fanaticism. My office became a sort of field headquarters, with daily meetings and reports, new plans concocted, successes or failures registered. As the struggle went on, we secured some new concessions—certain categories of Jews to be exempt from deportation: former soldiers in French armies or their families; the very aged and the ill; parents whose children were French citizens.

But almost before the ink was dry on a Vichy promise of exemption we would discover that it was worthless. One week in Vichy I was assured that in no case would ex-soldiers in French and Allied armies be touched. Just a few days later in Marseilles I learned that some of our Czechoslovaks, men who had risked their lives to fight at the side of the French, men who had been left in France because they were too close to the front to escape when the main Czech army was evacuated to England in June, 1940, were being held in concentration camps awaiting deportation. I at once telephoned Vichy for an explanation. "Oh, well," I was told, "ex-soldiers—what does that mean? Some Jew who served in the quartermaster's department or a few months in a camp—he's not to be considered an ex-combatant."

Ilot K in Les Milles had become the last station before loading the deportation trains. Refugees from all over that corner of France were sent to Les Milles to be "processed" and those selected for the next transport went into Ilot K. Here a young French pastor, leader of the resident CIMADE-YMCA team, played an important role, until the moral problem surrounding the selection of those for the transports became too onerous. The police order for each transport would simply specify the number of Jews to be taken. It was then left to camp management to make the selection. For the early deportation groups the pastor would review the proposed lists with the camp director, pleading or arguing for this or that person. But as it became evident that removal of one man from the list, however justifiable, simply condemned some other to be taken, the pastor found it impossible to continue these efforts.

In the meantime an aroused Western world began to bombard Vichy with cables of protest. If Pétain's Foreign Office had felt itself more or less isolated from the West because of its collaboration with Hitler, it was now suddenly a center of attention. Alerted by local representatives of our Nîmes organizations and by the press, many governments and hundreds of private agencies added their influence to what we continued doing in France.

The National Council of the Reformed Church of France met and ordered a message read from all pulpits: "The Church cannot further remain silent in face of the sufferings of thousands of human beings who have received asylum on our soil. The Church would have lost its soul and its reason for existence if it did not maintain that divine law is above all human contingencies. And this divine law does not permit that families created by God be broken up, children separated from mothers, the right of asylum and its compassion be unrecognized, the respect for the human person be transgressed, and beings without defense be delivered to tragic fates."

Whether or not as the result of such protests, Vichy now reluctantly granted permission to OSE to move 1,200 children from occupied France to their children's colonies in the south. These were some of the children left behind in northern France when their parents had been taken to Poland. The Joint Distribution Committee reported to its New York office: "These children, orphaned for at least the duration, will be brought to safety in southern France, where they can receive adequate care." Care was one thing; safety, as we were soon to discover, was quite another.

We never knew what motivated the Germans to allow these orphans to leave occupied territory: some thought it was a matter of shrinking food supplies in the north; another story had it that someone had bribed a high Nazi official. In any case, a few weeks later the Nazis were trying, vainly, to take these youngsters for deportation.

Joint action of Coordination Committee members obtained Laval's promise not to touch children in homes and colonies conducted by our relief agencies. In consequence, the agencies were besieged with requests to take in more children. Frantic parents, themselves facing probable deportation, thought they might at least save their children from the Nazi terror. A few weeks later Laval's promise to us was revealed to be as treacherous as the rest of his words and actions. With horrified fascination we watched the Nazi action pattern unfold: first a finger was seized, then the hand, then the whole arm, each time with the assurance that the victim should be grateful that no larger bite was taken.

The children's camp at Rivesaltes had already received four thousand Jewish children suddenly transferred from occupied France, piled in atop the large number of children with parents already in residence. Now, as our agencies acted on Vichy's consent to remove children from the camp to colonies and homes, another harrowing situation arose. Parents of children under eighteen were granted the choice of leaving their children in France to be cared for by strangers or taking them along to share the common fate. This announcement created new agony: few human families are more closely linked than the Jews. Nights of agonizing debates followed frantic efforts to communicate with some family connection outside the camp for counsel. In hundreds of cases the mother had to face this decision alone, the father having been taken eastward or held in some foreign labor group. Often the children themselves would be brought into the discussion. In most cases the decision was to leave children behind.

No one slept the night before the children were to be moved out of the camp, now almost entirely occupied by men and women whose fate was sealed. Those hours remain an ineffaceable memory. Some groups, both Christian and Jewish, spent the night in prayer. Some parents passed hours writing out final admonitions for their children: many wrote wills, disposing of property they had left in Germany, for the youngsters to take with them. The terrible morning came, with the military trucks drawn up before the office. Families clung to each other—many cried out in wild affliction and others stood dry-eyed and tense as children were loaded into the trucks. We would never forget the moment when the vehicles rolled out of camp, with parents trying in one last gaze to fix an image to last for eternity.

twenty-one

FIVE THOUSAND VISAS

Iɴ ᴠɪᴄʜʏ ɪ ʜᴀᴅ sᴜɢɢᴇsᴛᴇᴅ ᴛᴏ
Marshal Pétain that the United States might admit children
threatened with deportation from France. The idea had come
out of our emergency committee meetings, and some preliminary steps had already been taken before I saw Pétain.

We in Marseilles knew that our corresponding organizations
in the States were already raising the question in Washington.
Could not some thousands of emergency visas be authorized,
in any form whatever, to move these threatened children out
of danger? If such visas were granted, we could bring pressure
on Laval to grant the corresponding exit permits.

A fortnight after my visit to Pétain Vichy had announced
that parents to be deported would have no choice: their children would accompany them. Laval stated that these "anti-

Semitic measures will be taken only against foreign Jews, and these measures will be applied as ordered." He added that this was "a simple measure of purging out the unassimilable foreign Jews who clutter the black markets and engage in anti-Pétain and pro-de Gaulle campaigns."

From Marseilles the JDC representative cabled his New York office on September 5: "Eighty children from camp Les Milles whose parents left previously were deported yesterday. Five thousand others now in Rivesaltes immediately threatened. Urgent you make every effort to emigrate as many of these as possible. American organizations have cabled Mrs. Roosevelt asking her interest. Every minute counts now." And later the same day: "In addition ten thousand (adults) already deported from unoccupied France, another seven thousand scheduled to go next days. . . . Arrests being made in all cities. Children being removed from institutions supported by private philanthropy, including Swiss Red Cross. Push U.S. visas for largest number possible."

But would Vichy go along with this plan? Facing Laval's reluctance and the certainty that even if exit visas were granted the operation might take months, the JDC in New York, early in September, suggested that we explore the possibility of moving children first to Switzerland "under appropriate guarantee of maintenance during temporary stay." And on September 10 New York cabled: "Hope have all permissions immigration one thousand refugee children within ten days. Work out administrative responsibility for selection, visas, transportation, etc. U.S. Committee willing waive restrictions against children with relatives here."

That same day, however, we cabled New York: "Exit visa situation now much worse and for present practically impossible even for Jews of French nationality to obtain exit permits. All plans must be held in abeyance temporarily." We also reported that both Swiss and Portuguese authorities were being approached again concerning possible movement of children to those countries for a temporary sojourn, but that we had small hope of such permission unless we could guarantee that children would move on to other countries within a short time. All organizations, we told New York, were engaged in all possible preliminary preparations, but could undertake no actual processing of children "until we have government decision on number of children it will accept."

Then came the exciting news that the State Department agreed to admit a thousand children and on September 18 had cabled the Marseilles consulate instructions to issue the visas (noting that the Enemy Alien Act excluded children over twelve born in Germany or Austria, thus protecting America from subversive influences). But the same day the *Times* man in Vichy reported an interview with Laval: "No man and nothing can sway me from my determination to rid France of foreign Jews and send them back to where they originated. I will take no lessons in humanitarianism from any country."

To intensify our efforts, I went at once to Geneva where, a month earlier I had helped organize a special Emergency Committee to work on obtaining visas from countries other than the United States. In Geneva we called on diplomatic representatives of all the likely countries—Canada, Mexico, and some of the other Latin-American republics. It was almost like an auction. To the ambassador of Country X I could say, "If Country Y is offering visas to save five hundred children, surely your government can do as much."

Professional diplomats, never known for their capacity to make haste, in this case outdid themselves. By this time the outside world was aware of the plight of Jews in France and soon Mexico offered 250 visas, Ecuador 200, Uruguay 500, and the Argentine 1,000. Crowded little Switzerland offered to accept an undetermined number of children. Before the operation had to be abandoned, the total of visas available was three times the number we had asked for.

Our preliminary estimate of the cost of the operation reached astronomical figures. However, Jewish agencies were prepared to give the necessary financial guarantees, and our efforts were not retarded one day by money considerations. New York cabled us in Marseilles that six doctors, ten nurses and twenty-five escorts were being recruited for the transport. We began to assemble details New York requested about shipboard accommodation, life belts adjusted for children, and time required for processing.

In the meantime Vichy police continued to arrest Jews in both parts of France. On the Riviera, where most well-to-do non-French Jews were living, there was panic. In one night there were five suicides. Another night the police raided an OSE home, arresting all adolescents. The next night they returned and took away the younger children.

New York informed us that the American Friends Service Committee was authorized to certify children presented for visas: "Quota visas for most, visitors' visas for others." We in Marseilles pleaded for visitors' visas only: "Under the existing regulations, and with present consular staff in Marseilles, it would take eight months to process the quota visas. Lowrie is now in Vichy working on French exit permits."

On September 24 a New York cable to the American consulate stated that the United States Committee would be required to act *in loco parentis*, to give the legal parents' permission for emigration. With most of these imperiled children either already orphans, or about to become so, the instruction seemed superfluous.

Faced with the actual possibility of letting a thousand children escape their designs, Vichy bureaucrats now gave grudging consent for five hundred children only. I knew all too well the seesaw of influences in Vichy, so we did not despair of obtaining more visas, but at once went to work on the first five hundred.

The cable we sent New York reporting that Vichy was granting only five hundred visas "deferring action on others until later," prudently insisted: "This must not occasion publicity of any sort hostile to the Germans." However, publicity was inevitable and the French government, angered by unfavorable reports in the American press, was reconsidering the whole matter, meanwhile authorizing no exit visas. We reported to New York that processing of children was proceeding nevertheless and that several hundred United States visas could be issued, once Vichy made up its mind.

Most of the personnel of all the chief agencies in Marseilles had been mobilized to assist the Quakers in preparing a thousand children for presentation to the Consulate. Given an entry visa into the United States, we foresaw no serious difficulty with transit visas, Spanish and Portuguese, though the Spanish could be terribly deliberate in matters concerning Jews. Friends in Lisbon wrote me that the Portuguese would issue visas in blocks, and we hoped the Spanish authorities might agree to the same procedure. The agencies had set up a careful organization to assure the speediest possible processing, once French exit permits had been granted. First, youngsters from children's homes near Marseilles would be called, and a fixed schedule would order the reception of those from other places afterward.

Preparing children for emigration was no simple matter. Even the selection was complicated. With a thousand places and two thousand applicants all eagerly presenting their almost equal claims, how do you choose? What do you do if two children of the same family have different nationalities, one having been born in Prague and the other in Lyon? What do you do with a child whose parents have been deported and who has lost all his identity papers? Medical examinations and inoculations must be carefully scheduled. A full history of each child must be recorded, for use in eventual placement in the States.

On October 5 Sumner Welles informed the chairman of the United States Committee: "The President authorizes me to inform you that he approves a decision to grant visas to five thousand instead of one thousand in France. He does not believe it desirable, however, that any public statement about this decision be made." The Committee replied that in order to bring five thousand children into the United States it would have to raise five million dollars, so some kind of public statement in America would have to be made about the President's decision. Such publicity would have to be a calculated risk. That same week a United Press dispatch from Vichy reported that Laval had informed the United States Embassy there that France would grant exit visas to five thousand children. This seemed too good to be true, as it later turned out to be.

The New York *Times* of October 15 reported from Vichy: "The United States Committee for the Care of European Children, which has raised a $900,000 relief fund, has posted bond in Philadelphia for one thousand Jewish children from France. The bond guarantees that they will not become public charges. . . . American consuls have received authorization to issue emergency visas. Don Lowrie, representing the American Relief Committee at Geneva, will arrive Saturday to discuss details with Laval's Secretary-General."

On October 18 a delegation of the Quakers, in charge of moving children to the States, met me in Vichy. Our main business was to bargain with the reluctant authorities for exit permissions for one thousand, instead of five hundred, children and the speediest possible procedures thereafter. The United States chargé d'affaires, Mr. Pinckney Tuck, an old friend, had taken the greatest interest all through this visa struggle, and again gave us his full support. After two high-pressure conversations with high-ranking officials we got what we wanted. But minor bureaucrats were rarely generous in promising simplified technical measures, and I cabled home only that "the operation is beginning at once, and we hope to have the whole thousand on the ocean before Christmas."

For a fortnight we worked and waited for Vichy to send the authorizations to Marseilles, but continued with preparations as though we were sure of the outcome. By the last week in October we had completed all arrangements, assured railroad passage across Spain and Portugal, and had chartered a ship from Lisbon. At last I was informed by the Marseilles Prefecture that authorization to issue up to five hundred visas had been received from Vichy. On November 7 the group of twenty-three escorting personnel, pediatricians and trained child-care workers sailed from New York for Lisbon.

The next day the Allies landed in North Africa, and the Germans swept into complete occupation of France. On the 12th this cable went to New York: "All train service for civilians suspended. Possibilities for departure now practically nonexistent." And on the 13th, "All emigration from France to the United States now stopped. Have canceled all transportation arrangements."

This ended another chapter, or rather several chapters at once, for persons and organizations and the whole story of the war. For the past three weeks the Nazis had been so busy collecting workmen, French and foreign, for their industry in Germany that the deportations had almost completely stopped. Here and there Jews were being seized and sent to Rivesaltes, but the general atmosphere was calmer. Life in refugee camps had returned to something approaching normal, and all our Nîmes agencies had paused for a bit to prepare for whatever might lie ahead. Some of us had felt we might risk taking a short breathing spell, and we had set our next Nîmes Committee ahead a month so that we might have the time.

Helen and I had gone to Geneva, and from there on November 1 went down to Locarno for a proposed ten-day rest. The next morning my Geneva office had telephoned news of the Allied landing in North Africa and the German occupation of southern France. So we hurried back to Geneva. On November 10 the United States broke off all diplomatic relations with Vichy, and it was clear that the two of us were to remain in Switzerland for the duration.

For most of our American colleagues, however, a less agreeable chapter was opening. As far back as April the United States Embassy had requested all Americans not engaged in urgent business in unoccupied France to return home, but the representatives of all our relief agencies had chosen to remain at their jobs, and the Embassy had approved our decision. Consequently, when southern France was occupied, the Germans took all the Americans they could find, mostly diplomatic and relief personnel, and transferred them for what proved to be over a year's internment in Baden-Baden.

The sheer chance of our having chosen this moment to be in Switzerland saved the Lowries from that long Baden-Baden vacation, and it was with rather mixed feelings that, pursuing our usual tasks, I was soon forwarding from our YMCA office in Geneva to my fellow Americans in Baden-Baden books, musical instruments and theatrical material, just as we had been doing for the internees in France.

Changing headquarters from Marseilles to Geneva meant no lessening of work to be done. For one thing, we still had those five thousand U.S. visas, or the promise of them. Could they not be used to save the children, even if overseas travel was out of the question?

For some reason, and contrary to their policy in occupied territory, the Germans at their first entry into southern France, did not deport children under sixteen. Later it became known that their intention was to turn all these youngsters into good Nazis as replacements for the terrible losses of German men in the war. On January 14, 1943, in a cable to New York I suggested: "Urge effort to get countries originally granting visas to assure validity after war. Chance that Swiss might admit them in this case." Since most of the countries concerned were at war, and some of them felt they already had all the Jewish immigration they could manage, this was no simple matter. Formal visas, valid until after the end of hostilities, or some sort of gentlemen's agreement between certain American countries and Switzerland, had to be arranged. Swiss neutrality and other international questions complicated the undertaking.

As we anticipated, the Swiss authorities took the position that to admit (and feed and house) such a large number of

children, no private assurances that the youngsters would be
moved to other countries after the war would be acceptable:
there must be guarantees by a responsible government. At the
other side of the Atlantic the State Department pointed out
that such a guarantee could not be given since it would involve binding a future administration to issue visas to children
who by that time might be adults. The Bermuda Conference
on Refugees, currently in progress, helpfully suggested a
joint declaration to the neutral nations by the Allied governments pledging that after the war they would return to their
respective homelands all refugees forced by persecution to
leave. The suggestion appeared to have been accepted, but
nothing of practical value for our problem resulted.

In November of 1943 I received a letter (uncensored) in
Geneva reporting that the Germans had "blocked" all Jewish
children's homes and that their French leaders were arranging
to dissolve these centers and "lodge children with private
families." A JDC memo can go on with the story of our Emergency Committee: "The Swiss government was persuaded
to approach Vichy authorities to permit the children to leave
France via Spain. This request of the Swiss government,
which was based entirely upon humanitarian grounds, was refused by the French. Nevertheless, we continued to press the
Swiss government to make a second démarche to the effect
that Switzerland herself would be prepared to give asylum to
the children. Switzerland continues to request the formal guarantee of re-evacuation."

If we could secure the revalidation of at least some of these
visas, there was a chance of slipping some children across the
border. A confidential "note" I sent the Swiss Minister of
Foreign Affairs at that time outlined our approach.

"Beginning with August, 1942, the anti-Semitic persecution
initiated a special campaign against children. After the mass
deportation of adults in Paris, more than four thousand children were left to wander in the streets or weep before the
sealed doors of their former homes. . . . A few days later

they were loaded into trains, sixty to a car, the doors were sealed shut . . . and no one has heard of them since . . . .

"At the beginning of January, 1943, the German authorities introduced a new system of control . . . Jewish children's homes were blocked . . . so that any movement or change of address was forbidden. At the end of January, eight hundred of these children were deported under the same conditions as in 1942. Since then, another 'blocked' home near Marseilles, with thirty children whose parents had been deported, has been under direct supervision of the German police. On October 20 they, together with the directress and her assistant, were deported. During this operation the Germans took sixty hostages, to prevent any attempt at escape.

"It now appears that in the immediate future all children's homes in the former nonoccupied zone will be 'blocked' in the same manner. Thus about two thousand more children are threatened with deportation, orphans whose parents have already been deported. . . . If, despite all police measures, only six or seven thousand children have been taken, it is because the greater part of the others have been removed from danger . . . thanks to rescue work organized by private organizations of all faiths and political colors, eminent personalities of the churches and a large part of the general population.

"It is now evident that . . . the capacity to take children into families has reached the saturation point (this was an exaggeration—but it strengthened our argument) and that thus several thousand other children will be 'blocked' in homes, under the menace of deportation. Some of these have succeeded in passing into Spain, others into Switzerland. But about 1500 are left whose lives practically depend on one thing: the possibility of entering Switzerland within the next few weeks. At the moment, further passage into Spain is impossible. Up to now, Swiss authorities have never refused mission to a single child, but it would be quite understable if Switzerland should feel that it cannot accept an unlimited number of foreign children.

"The Geneva Emergency Committee which last year obtained five thousand emigration visas for these children, visas made useless by the German occupation, is doing its utmost to assure the validity of these visas, once the war is ended.

"The immediate question is whether the Swiss authorities should issue formal authorization for the thousand or fifteen hundred children there is still time to save . . . or let things remain as they are, risking the chance that entry may be refused" (November 15, 1943).

I do not recall that a reply was ever received to this note, but neither do I know of a refugee child's being refused entry into Switzerland.

Another proposition partly evolved by our Emergency Committee in Geneva, which dragged through several months, was that the British government should arrange with the Palestinian government to reserve for these children a sufficient number of the 30,000 immigration certificates for Palestine already authorized but unusable because of the war. Both British and United States governments associated themselves with this proposal, but nothing came of it. On request of the State Department (December 23, 1943) the JDC reaffirmed the guarantee given earlier to the United States Committee for maintenance of five thousand children if permitted entry into the United States.

During these months our Geneva Committee, in concert with similar committees in the other countries concerned, was trying to secure the revalidation of the visas each country had originally offered, making them good until some indefinite future date. Although this was a proposition quite without precedent in diplomatic history, most of the countries we approached eventually gave the necessary assurance, and these were communicated to Berne, but no final action was taken and the matter remained in suspense until the close of hostilities.

Fairly accurate lists now showed six thousand children left in France who had to remain in hiding until the American troops stormed up the Rhône valley to liberate them, together with all their French protectors.

twenty-two

THE CARDINAL'S
CHILDREN

THE CAMP AT VÉNISSIEUX, IN
the hill country three or four miles southeast of Lyon, witnessed one of the most exciting adventures in saving children.
This was a new camp created by the Germans almost a year
after they occupied southern France. A railroad spur ran
close by the camp, making it convenient for its special function as a transit point. Jews taken in a street *rafle* or in a midnight descent on some residence section were brought to
Vénissieux and held there until a trainload could be collected.
Even though their military transport problem was already
causing headaches, the Germans somehow found trains for
the deportations, and persons in Vénissieux usually remained
there for only a short time, sometimes a few hours. Then they
were packed into the boxcars and dispatched eastward.

As a new camp, Vénissieux showed several distinctive features. Perhaps because of the lack of barbed wire or because the Germans could not spare time for more elaborate construction, the Vénissieux camp was confined by only one circle of wire instead of the double or triple encirclement used at Gurs or Vernet. But, unlike the older camps, this one fence carried a powerful electric current. Any attempt to pass it meant death.

The German guard company recruited from Hitler's last call-up, clearly reflected another shortage. By this time only old men scarcely fit for field duty and beardless boys were available. The guard at Vénissieux was made up of men too old to be fanatic Nazis, under the command of one Sergeant Braun, barely twenty but truly a "Hitler youth," conscious of Nazism's mission to cleanse Europe of Jews. Sergeant Braun may have been already discouraged at the progress of the war or perhaps he was too lonely among the oldsters; in any case he was reported as being fairly drunk most of the time.

Again, unlike other camps, Vénissieux permitted no relief work by any of our agencies. In fact, even visitation by "Nîmes" people was forbidden: only chaplains had access to the camp. And, instead of being a camp principally for men or for children, as Les Milles and Rivesaltes had become, whole families were interned at Vénissieux. Now that most foreign Jews had been deported, these families were French, as Nazi fanaticism overrode all previous agreements and promises to Marshal Pétain.

Virtually a shipping yard and nothing more, Vénissieux provided no sorting pen, no lists to be combed over and discussed by relief agencies or pastors. Once people were in this camp there was no chance that any outsider might intervene to secure their release or stay. These people were doomed.

Because of this desperate situation an urgent conference of Christian agencies, both Protestant and Catholic, was held at Chambon. Most of the CIMADE leaders were there, and a representative group of Catholics. Two main topics were up for discussion: tactics and conscience. In response to the increasing babarity of the Nazis, how far could Christians go in illegality? Might violence be countered with violence? Christians were constantly risking their lives in passage to Switzerland or in the clandestine transport of children—could salvage efforts go so far as to risk German lives? The Maquis was quietly "liquidating" German guards or small town garrisons—how far should Christians go, along this path of warfare, if the effort was to save Jewish lives?

Apparently, no final limits were set, but there was general agreement that the time had come to spare no effort, however perilous, if thereby some might be saved. The old techniques of extracting inmates still served pretty well in what was left of the older camps, although there, too, German guards had begun to replace the French police, but Vénissieux presented a different problem.

Before many days had passed, Vénissieux became an actual and no longer a theoretical problem. In a new wave of arrests the Nazis had taken well-known Jewish families from Marseilles and Lyon and the Riviera and shipped them to Vénissieux. Among those seized were leaders of some of our Nîmes organizations, personal friends and acquaintances. For some reason most of this leadership group had been spared before. A half-dozen Christian leaders quickly got together in the CIMADE headquarters in Lyon to consider a course of action.

They debated various schemes. Could the Maquis be asked to overwhelm the German guards and let the entire camp scatter into the countryside? Even if this plan should succeed, it would mean massive reprisals against all remaining Jews in France and anyone else suspected of being implicated. Anyway, with German occupation troops everywhere, the whole vicinity of the camp could be blocked off and only a few of the escapees would be able to elude the thorough search that would surely follow.

Another proposal offered better chances of success: to wait until the train was loaded, and at a certain point derail it. Not far from the camp the railway climbed a steep hill on a curve. Part of this curve was in a deep cut, and then the track came out on a level space. Trains starting from the camp would take this curve very slowly, and some of the planners thought that if it could be stopped just here some children at least, if parents had been instructed beforehand, could leap from the cars, run out on the level grade, and be picked up in the resulting confusion. A truck or two would be waiting on a little-used road that ran quite close to the spot, and the children could be whisked away while the train guards were trying to find out what had happened. Inside information from the camp would let the plotters know when the train was to leave, and action could be timed for the right moment.

With the proper tools it would be easy, they thought, to unbolt one end of a rail and pry it out of line. One of the Protestant leaders knew how to procure railroad workers' tools. But then they began to question the wisdom of this plan. None of them had any experience in wrecking trains. Suppose the train was running faster than usual? Suppose a car should overturn on leaving the tracks? They decided derailment would not do. They must think of something else.

I heard the rest of the story from Mlle. B., one of the Protestant leaders. Because she was visiting camps near Marseilles on the day of that council of war, she could not reach Lyon in time to participate. But soon after she reached Lyon she met the Abbé G., one of the Catholic leaders in the Nîmes Committee. He told her they had decided on "a very risky chance" to break through the single wire fence at Vénissieux and help some children to escape.

"I visited the camp this morning," the Abbé told her, "and looked over the ground again, and I believe our plan is worth trying. It was a great temptation to tell at least a few leaders that we'd be coming in tonight, and we have had some anxious discussions on this point. It would be much easier if we were expected. Some argued that it would be unfair not to warn parents in advance, but we had to decide against it. You know how swiftly rumors spread in a camp, and we were afraid someone might inadvertently give the secret away."

The two agreed to meet at the town's Café de la Paix at eleven o'clock that night. Arrived there, Mlle. B. noticed several other Nîmes friends, but neither she nor the Abbé gave any sign of recognition. As they slipped quietly toward the camp about midnight (there was no moon, and it was very dark) Abbé G. explained what they were going to do:

"You know the wire fence around the camp is electrified, so no one dares to climb it. And for this reason all the guards usually sit in the warmth of the gatehouse, not troubling to patrol the fence. At midnight the power cable to the camp will be cut. One of our men is a professional linesman, and he knows the place where the camp power line branches off from the trunk cable, so he knows just where to operate. Then we cut the fence and go in to gather all the children we can, in the few minutes before the Nazis find out what is going on. We'll work in pairs: I will be wearing my cassock to give people confidence, and you are to do most of the talking. I've been there enough times to know a clear path to the fence; we can do this in the dark."

Each had rubber gloves, a flashlight and pliers. There were dim lights in a few of the barracks as they cautiously approached the wire, but most of them were dark and quiet, as though everyone was asleep.

"Our section is over here on the east side," the Abbé told Mlle. B., and about the time they reached the fence at that point all the lights in the camp went out.

As they started cutting the barbed wire, making a hole large enough to step through easily with a child, the Abbé pointed. "The three barracks nearest here, F, G, and H, are ours."

All at once they could hear people stirring in the barracks. They slipped into the nearest one, in darkness like Egypt, and began talking to people they could feel, in their beds, or already sitting up.

"Do you have children?" they would ask, seizing a woman's

hand. "We represent the Christian churches of France, and
have come to save them. After the war you can have them
again: the Cardinal of Lyon himself guarantees it. Here is the
Abbé, his representative."

By some sort of miracle no one screamed. Everyone spoke
in whispers. It was almost as though the invaders had been
expected. They used their flashlights to show the Abbé in his
clericals, but only for this. Once or twice a mother hesitated
or refused, and they passed on to the next cot: time was being
counted in seconds.

As fast as they would be given one or two children, they
would put them through their hole in the fence and tell them
to lie perfectly still until they came again. Mlle. B. said afterward they should have had a third person at the fence, because
one or two of the small children began to cry, and they had
to tie a handerkchief over one four-year-old's mouth.

The tension was frightening. Here were parents in the darkness of midnight suddenly confronted with the decision to put
their children into the hands of strangers, with the only guarantee the Abbé in his soutane and the whispered promises of
the two workers—To wake a child from sleep for a separation
that might be forever. . . .

Soon they saw lights coming toward them from the direction of the guardhouse, and heard the Germans crying, "*Was
ist los?*" That meant that their raid was finished. Mlle. B. and
the Abbé had eight children outside the fence, and they hustled
them off to a side road where two big German military buses
were waiting, motors running. It was only then that Mlle. B.
discovered that she and the Abbé were one of twelve teams,
each at a different spot along the wire. Altogether they had a
hundred children. The bus drivers were members of a French
Catholic organization, wearing German uniforms. And they
pulled away before any light came on in the camp.

They drove directly to a convent in the Fourvière suburb
of Lyon. The sisters were expecting them. Within an hour
after the wire had been cut, all the Cardinal's children were

in safety.

But a hundred children could not be housed permanently even in the largest convent in Lyon. So, one or two at a time, children were taken on a train journey, or for a ride in one of the rare cars the relief agencies could still operate. Mostly they were hidden in the farming country west of Lyon, or in the Catholic boarding schools. Three schools near Lyon could accept groups instead of individuals. In other towns the local pastor or the curé would have a list of people he knew would receive a child, and this helped the eventual dispersal. Sometimes, because of the need for quick action, an agency representative and his charges arrived at a boarding school on very short notice, and never once were they refused.

Here, for almost the first time in the complicated story of hiding children, the problem of identification arose. The need to be able, after the war, to return children to their families had been the constant concern of our agencies. Some of the children from Vénissieux were too small to know much about themselves, and of course no data could be collected during the raid, save an occasional whispered, "Her name is ————." An attempt was made to place most of the nameless ones in families, in order better to preserve their individuality. Later, by talking with the older children or by tracing a bit of marked clothing, some of the little ones could be identified, but some never were. At the end of the war they were placed in charge of the OSE or other Jewish agencies. As far as we know, none of those Vénissieux parents returned after the war to claim their children from the Cardinal.

twenty-three

HIDING SIX
THOUSAND CHILDREN

Aｌｍｏｓｔ ｄａｉｌｙ ｔｈｅ ａｇｅｎｃｉｅｓ
managed to extract a few dozen children from the camps,
sometimes with genuine documents permitting their transfer
to an OSE home or to a Quaker colony, sometimes by less
legal methods.

A group of thirty children would leave the Rivesaltes camp
on a hike, and only fifteen would return. The others "had run
away in the town." Some youngsters were sent on doctors'
orders (genuine) to a nonexistent children's clinic in Marseilles. The address given was the Unitarian Service Committee's dispensary for adults, but it served the purpose. One
friendly delivery man had a secret compartment built under
the seat of his truck, which could contain two or three small
children and allow them breathing space until, outside the
camp, they could be transferred to a car waiting on a side
road and rushed to a home ready to receive them. Again, it
was largely thanks to friends in the camp administration and
the local police force that such operations were possible.

As a matter of fact, most of the population of southern France was alert and ready to help threatened children. Whether out of love for youth or hatred for the enemy occupants, most local authorities, as well, worked hand in glove with our agencies in this vast game of hide and seek.

For greater security, the agencies set up an elaborate organization, almost like a business enterprise, of acquisition and delivery of goods. To minimize risks, they divided the whole of southern France into separate compartments, each operating largely on its own, while one or two leaders maintained contact with all the other sectors. Thus in case of a misstep, or a brush with the German police in one sector, no trails leading to other sectors could be followed by the Nazis. The occupants, of course, suspected this, and their action toward all workers for refugees took forms that might have been expected.

Maintaining thousands of children in hiding was a huge enterprise. First Christian parents had to decide to take upon themselves and their own children the risk of taking in a Jewish child, and Laval had proclaimed that hiding a Jew was an act of treason. Then a child had to be selected who more or less naturally fitted into a given family picture. If he was to be presented as a member of this family he had to be of the right age and, if possible, the right complexion.

And then the youngster selected had to be brought, sometimes halfway across southern France, to his sheltering family. In one place the same creaky wagonload of hay was used a dozen times to deliver a child to his adopting family. Of course, save for the big towns, no family could suddenly receive another five- or fifteen-year-old child, and keep it a secret. Concealment was a matter of village-wide conspiracy. The fact that no "leaks" occurred was due almost as much to hatred of the Nazis as to the common effort to save children's lives.

In any case, from that moment on, not only did the parents have to prevaricate, but they also had to teach their own children to lie: "This is our cousin Auguste from Stras-

bourg . . ." Families had to have extra ration cards, but
these could easily be fabricated. In most villages the shopkeepers cooperated. The adopted youngsters also had to have
"proper" identity papers. One parish set up a complete coun-
terfeiting apparatus. Since most of the youngsters had lost
their "cartes d'identité," local officials would often issue
substitutes.

The police could not give all their attention to hunting
children, because all French manpower—and "man" began
at fifteen—was being rounded up and transported to Germany
for wartime employment. This circumstance had mixed reper-
cussions on the shelter projects for children. In hundreds of
cases a French family with a son over fifteen was hiding him
as well as a foreign child. In the best "hideout" sections of
France, west and southwest from Lyon and in the Cévennes
(where Chambon is located), what with families hiding their
own sons and the fact that this was officially designated as a
reception area for evacuees from bombed coastal defense
zones, "the absorptive capacity" as it was called, was almost
exhausted. On the other hand, this generous immixture of
outsiders made changes in each family less conspicuous.

Once twenty-five or forty children were safely tucked
away in some village you were never sure how long you might
be able to keep them there. Almost everywhere we had inside
information about imminent action by the police—a given
area was to be blocked while a new house-to-house search
was carried out. Sometimes a hundred children had to be
moved in a night, smuggled through the police cordons into
some other areas. Sometimes the new area was a place that
had been carefully surveyed and prepared, months before, to
receive more children; sometimes temporary overcrowding
of a section already near the saturation point had to be risked.
In most places the local police were now altogether on our
side. It was not uncommon for them to arrest and imprison
temporarily a young Frenchman being hunted by the Nazis
for their work gangs in the Reich.

The whole operation was a joint effort by Jewish and

Christian organizations, mostly OSE and ORT and, on the Christian side, CIMADE and the Catholic institutions. Protestants did not have many places that could be used for storage of a whole group of children at a time, as the Catholics did. For instance, a group of young Protestant conspirators in Grenoble planned to "kidnap" forty Jewish children from the fortress where they were being held, scheduled for deportation eastward the following day. With the aid of some French authorities they arrived at the fortress gates one midnight with two trucks and forged papers authorizing them to move the children to another prison. The Vichy police never could trace those two truckloads of children, who went directly into a convent school in the city. A few days later our committee looked them over and, one by one, they were taken into private homes.

As the summer of 1943 advanced, this secret organization in France could be consolidated. Soon assistants trained in social case work and approved by the various relief bodies were attached to special staffs operating in each of the sectors. Despite the difficulties and grave dangers of travel, at regular intervals they would visit the children in hiding, overhaul their wardrobes, and check on their state of health and their schooling.

By January 1, 1944, twenty-five such special workers were operating, working under the leadership of one director in each sector who was responsible for the application of general rules concerning welfare, and for the coordination of all activities on the children's behalf. At the beginning of this year three thousand children had been registered in three sectors independent one from the other, and fresh contingents of children were being regularly taken into hiding. In addition, some two thousand children were hiding, together with their parents, scattered all over French territory. Soon the total passed the six thousand mark.

In Geneva the OSE headquarters built up a special catalogue of the children in both France and Switzerland. Each card carried the fingerprints of a child, both its real and its assumed name, and whenever possible a photograph. The data assembled for youngsters who had received United States visas in Marseilles in the autumn of 1942 provided a good beginning for the catalogue that eventually included five thousand names, a document of inestimable value when these children were liberated at the end of hostilities.

The great expense of this whole operation of concealment may be imagined. In addition to the cost of feeding and clothing six thousand children under these emergency conditions, in a country suffering the severest penury there was also the added expense of medical and dental care as well as the maintenance and travel costs of supervisory personnel. Fortunately the "available balance" system we used before 1943, and similar procedures, continued to function, so funds were made available; "Otherwise," as one worker put it, "this dangerous and delicate work would be compromised."

One report to the Intergovernmental Committee in 1944 concluded with this paragraph: "Attention is drawn to the fact that owing to the active sympathy of all the French relief organizations involved, the great devotion of the visiting personnel, and the sound character of the system adopted, not a single child has been lost hitherto."

And this almost miraculous record was continued until the war ended. There was one tragic mishap when the Nazis put their dogs on a small group of children being helped through the barbed wire on the Swiss frontier, and the whole group perished. The grave of the courageous young French woman guide was found after the war.

On September 6, 1944, we received a letter from a Jewish chaplain with the American forces advancing up the Loire valley. "This territory," he wrote, "has just been liberated. I have been here five days and every day some more Jewish children come out of hiding. One day five, the next eleven, and so on. There must be hundreds of kids scattered all over this territory, and they owe their lives to the courage of hundreds of Christian families."

twenty-four

CZECH AID
UNDER THE OCCUPATION

I<small>N</small> M<small>ARSEILLES</small> <small>IT TOOK THE</small>
occupying Germans nearly a month to turn their attention to
the Czech Aid. Early in the morning on December 3, 1942,
they occupied our offices, arresting all personnel as they came
to work. A neighbor warned one of the younger leaders
before he left his room and he succeeded in alerting one other,
the first assistant to the director. This man, one of whose half
dozen identity cards read "Dupont," took over the leadership
of Czech Aid.

Although hunted by the Gestapo for almost three years
after they had entered Marseilles, Dupont was able to elude
their clutches, largely because of his perfect alibi. Early in
the war, a French friend of his had fallen in battle, and the
young man's parents, deliberately neglecting to report his

death to French authorities, turned over to Dupont their
son's identity papers. By good fortune the young Frenchman
had almost exactly the same build and coloring as Dupont.
Having thus become a Frenchman (equipped with documents
proving he had recently returned from a German war prisoner
camp) Dupont could live without being challenged, at least
until the Germans began to impress all young men into work
groups. He was even able, on demand, to present documents
(genuine) proving that all four of his grandparents were
Aryan.

Thanks to the collaboration of officials in the University of
Aix, where he had been a student, our other young Czech
leader (he was just twenty) was able to change his identity
papers, and throughout the rest of the war ably seconded
Dupont under the name of Thurmond. All remaining staff
members were seized and transported first to a Paris prison,
where for weeks our friends could supply them with food
parcels, and thence to concentration camps in the Reich. The
Jewish members of the staff were never heard of afterward.
Of the others, one died in a German camp, but the rest, terribly
scarred by their experiences, lived through years of incarcera-
tion and returned to France after V-E Day.

Faced with constantly increasing danger, Dupont and
Thurmond were able to maintain practically all the Czech
Aid operations almost uninterrupted. For some months they
worked out of the YMCA office in the rue Pythéas, aided by
the French staff that was left. The YMCA had a good reputation with the Germans because of its world-wide services to
war prisoners in Britain, America and India, and nothing in
our Marseilles files would reveal any anti-German activity But
one day the Gestapo raided this office, incidentally giving
Thurmond the narrowest escape of all those exciting years.
As usual, the Gestapo broke into the office in the early morning. As each person, staff or caller, entered, a Nazi, revolver
in hand, would take him to a back room, search his pockets,
and warn him to remain silent and out of sight.

Among the early visitors that morning was Thurmond. Taking in the situation at first glance, he began at once to protest that he was a simple French student, come in to pick up some textbooks. Since our offices were always full of books, en route to or from the camps, this sounded plausible.

"What kind of books?"

The day before, Thurmond had laid out two books on agriculture, to be sent to the Lapeyre farm. "Books on agriculture," he told them. "I think they might be left for me on that desk."

"What do you know about this organization?" they demanded. Thurmond said he thought it must be a good institution since it supplied books to poor students.

The Germans had one Frenchman with them, and they turned the young Czech over to him for grilling. Fortunately Thurmond had graduated from the French Lycée in Prague before he came to the University of Aix. It is no small tribute to his command of the French language, as well as to his talent as an actor, that after a half hour of his sometimes tearful protests the Germans were convinced. They noted his name and address (both false), warned him of reprisals against his family if he told anyone of his arrest, and finally let him go. Thurmond at once alerted the remaining YMCA staff and posted a concealed guard to warn off any other visitors to the office.

When the Nazis got around to ransacking our office, a few hours later, they found some papers indicating that the frightened French student might have been who he really was, and from then on both Thurmond and Dupont worked with the knowledge that the Germans had offered a reward of 50,000 francs for information leading to their capture.

With both offices closed, the two young Czechs had to rely on helpful friends in Marseilles and across southern France. They rented a room in the house of a Czech workman in a Marseilles suburb to serve as headquarters for continuing operations.

Fortunately our faithful friends in the government apparatus in Vichy, principally in the Foreign Office, continued their support. After the closure of the Marseilles Czech Aid headquarters, a "Czech Office" was set up by "Foreign Affairs" to replace the consular functions the Czech Aid had carried. There was little of that type of work to do (our own men could and did fabricate almost any kind of document needed), but the new Czech agency served another useful purpose. It took possession of the Marseilles office and property of Czech Aid and turned them over, just as they had been put under seal by the Gestapo, to Dupont and the others who continued the work.

A paragraph from one of Dupont's reports at the end of 1943 tells the story: "Since the 'Office' offered only juridical and not material help, the 'Comité d'Assistance aux Réfugiés Tchèques' is proposed. This is supposed to be a private organization of seven people, friends of Czechoslovakia, which would conduct the social work hitherto done by the Centre d'Aide. It must be explained that officially the French know nothing of the fact that, although its property and offices were confiscated by the Gestapo, the Centre d'Aide still continues to function, underground. Vichy is insisting on the organization of this Committee for Aid of Czech Refugees, hence we shall have to comply with their suggestion. Since the lists of those helped by this Committee would be available to the Germans, we will take care that only those persons appear in the books who are too old or too ill to be in danger of being sent to Germany. We shall continue to care for all the others, as hitherto, in secret." Thurmond had persuaded the French postal officials to permit him, against all regulations, to copy the lists of earlier Czech Aid payments and was thus able to reconstitute those files, so that the Czechs never missed a month's payment of allowances.

The French accountant who, under my direction, had always audited the Czech Aid records, continued to do this with the accounts the two young men presented to him. All concerned, both the Czech government in London and we in Geneva, were amazed, once the war was ended, to receive a complete accounting for all Czech Aid financial operations right up to the date of the armistice.

The *de facto* Czechoslovak Minister in Geneva, Dr. Kopecky, was one of the most capable diplomats I ever encountered. He had been the Czechoslovak delegate to the League of Nations and had continued to live in Geneva after the collapse of that Wilsonian ideal, as official representative of the Czechoslovak Red Cross with the League of Red Cross Societies. Even after the Czechoslovak Republic had been crushed by the Nazi occupation, and despite German protests to the Swiss government, Dr. Kopecky maintained his office and full diplomatic privileges: an official car and the right to use the Czechoslovak language over the telephone. He was our only direct contact with President Beneš and the Czechoslovak government in London. From them he received funds to supplement what the American Friends of Czechoslovakia were sending me from New York. Money could be cabled to Switzerland; the problem was getting it into France.

This was sometimes effected by Monsieur Bertrand as he passed back and forth. Once Dupont came with him to Geneva. He had lost part of one trouser leg in getting his six-foot-four frame through the barbed wire at the frontier. It was not difficult to provide new pants, but for a pair of shoes large enough to replace his outworn footwear we had to scour the shoe stores in both Geneva and Berne. After Bertrand's arrest, Dupont visited me in Geneva a second time. On this trip he used another route, where there was no wire, but was somewhat concerned lest his enormous footprints in the snow might indicate to German border guards who had passed there.

Dupont told me how the Marseilles post office had agreed to deliver all mail addressed to the Czech Aid to the YMCA office and, after that was closed, to the secret headquarters outside town. Besides this, he had arranged postboxes in other villages. To one of these I had been instructed to send mail addressed to "Jean Montagnon." "Who is this Montagnon?" I asked Dupont.

"Oh, there are three of us," he explained, "each with an identity card in that name. In case anything should happen to one of us, another could receive the mail."

The closest call in Dupont's years of underground service to his fellow countrymen came one day when he was visiting the farm headquarters at Lapeyre. After our Nîmes Committee vice-president had lost that briefcase in the train, there were house searches as a result, but it took the Gestapo four months to discover Lapeyre. One night French neighbors reported that three cars "powered with gasoline" were prowling around the countryside: these could only belong to Germans. Hiding his bulging briefcase under a dog asleep in his kennel, Dupont and most of the other men left the house before dawn, retiring to the surrounding woods. The Germans took away two Jews who had come to the farm too late to be provided with the Bishop's "Orthodox" certificates. Then the visitors discovered the hidden briefcase with some of the counterfeit seals and stamps used in forging documents, together with all four of Dupont's identity cards, each bearing his photograph. Although they combed that region for days, Dupont's photo in hand, the Germans failed to catch him. If they had looked for a six-footer, the story might have been different, for Dupont was the tallest man in the province. Another reason for his escape was that Lapeyre lay at a point where three Gestapo administrative regions met, and Dupont moved over into another of our farms, a few miles away but in another region, where the police of that area never got around to searching for him.

After that German raid in Lapeyre, most of the Czech farmers not already away with the French underground lived with various of their neighbors, as did the director of the farms himself. Thus the farms could continue to operate under the disintegrating German control until American forces from the west rolled up over the Corrèze.

The children's colony at Vence ultimately had to move. When all of France was occupied, the southeast corner was taken by Italian troops instead of Germans. The Italians had no reason to dislike Czechs, and although they sometimes came up to see the children they made no move to interfere with the school's normal operation.

Even after the Germans took over, they did not disturb the children at Vence for several months. Then one day two German officers came and inspected the colony. They talked in German about what a pleasant place this would be for the General's residence. Vence was a village of artists; it had a marvelous view over the Mediterranean, and "look how well these Czechs are eating."

So the school's director was not surprised, a few days later, to receive a German army order to evacuate the school, "since it was needed for military purposes."

Much earlier, when we were just starting the Czech Aid, one of our compatriots had offered us the use of his château in the Creuse Department. At that time we could think of no use for it because it was too far off the main roads. The place was still available, and now it was decided to move the Vence project there.

Children and parents and cows and rabbits and hens, plus farm equipment and kindergarten furniture had to be moved three hundred miles to the northwest. At this time railroad transportation in France was nearly paralyzed, as Allied bombing destroyed more and more railroad material in Germany. But even the Germans couldn't put a hundred children out on the street. Since the General evidently liked the idea of living at Vence, it wasn't too difficult for us to get the railroad cars we needed. We moved everything we had in Vence, and we never lost a child or a cow.

And the colony's life flowed on, its only serious difficulties those of all of France in the last throes of the war. Most of the Vence children were not orphans, as were the majority of those in hiding, so after the end of the war they could rejoin their parents, and the Vence colony became only a pleasant memory.

Because we had planned the farms as one enterprise, the Czechs had less difficulty with food than most people in southern France. Registered as farmers, and because of their cordial relations with the French population, most of the men —and there were more than two hundred—on our eight farms continued working their land until that part of France was liberated by American forces and they could participate openly in the final rout of Hitler's armies. With the disappearance of the demarcation line, contact with northern France became possible, and several more camps were added to the list of those our farms were already serving with monthly food shipments. The crowded farmhouses also sheltered scores of Czechs who escaped from the German-controlled work gangs.

When the war was over, the lessors of our farms received back hundreds more acres of tillable land than they had had for fifty years, and properties in much better shape.

twenty-five

ALL CLEAR

Despite the tightened German controls on the Swiss-French frontier, we in Geneva were able to maintain considerable communication with southern France. Most of our Nîmes organizations, even some of the Jewish agencies, continued operation after the Germans had taken away all the American personnel. The occupants realized that these services were useful to them and, except in the case of Czechs and Poles, permitted the work to continue.

While some of the refugee camps had been closed and the population of the others was steadily diminishing through death and deportations, our devoted secretaries still continued to live inside the barbed wire, and to help these unfortunates as long as help was possible. Most of the needed supplies had to be sent from Switzerland, since France had been scraped bare by the occupying power. A postcard of acknowledgment from one bedridden internee in the camp at Noë said: "Thanks to the drawing material you sent, I can now forget everything around me."

One incident of Quaker service is worth telling here. The Quakers had learned that a train carrying two thousand Jews eastward would pass through Toulouse early one morning. Four women from the Quaker staff spent all night at the station, preparing to serve that train. There was one water faucet available, a half-mile from the yard where the train would stop. Mobilizing bottles, pails, anything else that would hold water, they were ready when the train pulled in: two thousand people already two days en route without food or drink, banging on the closed boxcar doors and crying for water. How could four women serve them all? The Quaker leader walked up to the Gestapo officer in charge. "You dare not let this train proceed before all these people have had at least a drink of water," she protested.

Another, older, officer supported her plea: "Don't you see these women are Quakers? They saved us Germans from starvation after the last war."

"What do you want?"

"We need help to carry water—there are only four of us."

The officer detailed a squad of soldiers to help, and the two thousand captives had food and water before the train moved off, probably the last touch of human sympathy before they reached Poland.

As the months of 1944 passed, all of us in Geneva followed the progress of the Allied armies in France with growing excitement and optimism. In August the drive up the Rhone valley brought American troops to the Swiss border, and I had my first sight of that strange vehicle we had been reading about, the jeep. With most of France now cleared of the enemy, our relief agencies, along with other pressing duties, could begin the task of regrouping the scattered Jewish children.

After the first days of liberation, some reported directly to
the rabbi with the American forces, and regrouping went on
in an orderly fashion. The OSE and the other Jewish agencies
reopened homes that had been evacuated to escape the Nazi
occupants. On November 11, 1944, OSE sent this cable from
Geneva to New York: "Have initiated action to reunite parents and children. Two thousand are receiving aid with
parents, three thousand are being placed in adoptive families
and children's homes."

Within a few weeks the thousand and more others hidden
in France had been located and brought under the care of the
Jewish agencies. All of us were surprised to discover that a
third of our hidden youngsters could be reunited with their
parents: the Christian organizations had done a larger job of
hiding adults than most of us had realized. Some families had
means to permit their entry into Switzerland from half-starved
France. Later they would return to the lands from which the
Nazis had driven them, Holland or Belgium or even Austria:
no one wanted to enter Germany again.

For the orphans the problems were different. In thousands
of homes the Jewish guest had become so much a part of the
family that separation now seemed unkind, almost impossible.
Christian families begged to be allowed to keep their charges
—offered to see them through school and even the university.
Some even advanced the claim that by sheltering a refugee
child at such a risk to themselves they had earned the right to
permanent adoption; and in most cases the child in question
was more than willing. But a child who became a full member
of a Christian family would probably grow up Catholic or
Protestant, and so be lost to the Jewish faith. Foster parents
promised to avoid all pressures in this direction, but even with
all possible guarantees the probability remained. There were
instances where Christian parents tried to keep the children,
regardless of the wish of the Jewish organizations. Newspaper
headlines followed one famous case that occupied the courts

for years, even involving extradition proceedings to recover children who had been smuggled out of France into Spain to escape a court decision that they must be released to Jewish sponsors. In the long run, however, practically all the orphaned children were taken into the care of OSE and the other Jewish groups.

Within the Jewish agencies themselves grave discussions continued. For almost every child there were many offers of adoption in the United States, families pleading to be allowed to bring these youngsters from tragedy-stricken Europe to the warmth of American homes. After long consideration of the problem it was decided that, save in cases of children with near relatives in America, youngsters should remain in Europe where Jewish families were equally eager to adopt them.

As the world returned gradually toward normal living, a group of over six hundred teen-agers was emigrated to Israel, there to become pioneers at developing agriculture in the new nation. On a visit to Israel five years later, one of the French Protestant leaders who had been most active in the wartime underground had the happy experience of renewing acquaintance with some of her Chambon protegées. I am sure we all had hoped that none of our hidden children would ever see the inside of a camp again, but for the teen-agers going to Israel a camp was set up near Marseilles, and today it serves as a transit point for Jews from North Africa on their way to Israel.

In Switzerland we continued our service in scores of camps. Swiss "camps" were usually in otherwise vacant hotels, without police guards or barbed wire, but the need for morale-building effort was almost as acute as in France. Thousands of these people had known our service in France, so that organizing the same in Switzerland was easy. The training courses we organized for the reconstruction work they would face as they returned to their homelands after the war were as popular as they were appropriate.

Besides service to foreigners, we two Americans were fortunate in being part of the YMCA prisoner-of-war service, which included assistance to thousands of our compatriots in German war prisoner camps. Helen organized an extensive program whereby American women in Switzerland wrote letters to American prisoners in Germany, particularly to men recently captured, as their names were fed into the Geneva office of the International Red Cross.

In January, 1945, I helped with the first exchange of invalid prisoners of war via Switzerland. As we had served men in all the camps, the YMCA served these men en route through this neutral country. We stationed a team of secretaries in Geneva and at Kreuzlingen, the frontier stations where exchanges took place. I was at Kreuzlingen and had the special privilege of accompanying two of the trains on the eight-hour trip to Geneva.

These returning prisoners represented all types and nationalities: ages twenty-one to forty; Canadians, Hindus, Negroes from the Sudan, New Zealanders, Channel Islanders, men from a dozen other parts of the British Empire, plus men from almost every state in the United States. They all wore soiled and shabby uniforms, since everyone had left most of his clothing with friends who still remained in camp.

What could you do for these men just emerging into liberty after months and years behind the barbed wire? The Swiss Red Cross gave them food, cigarettes, and hot water for washing; the American and British authorities were there to give a personal welcome; and the YMCA provided English illustrated weeklies, pencils, matches, pocket Testaments, and a special greeting card with a calendar on the back, besides putting into each train a couple of phonographs with records. It all seems very trivial, but to the men it was almost unbelievable. On a postcard one man asked me to mail back to his camp, I read: "The reception was tremendous. . . . We also received greetings from H.M. the King, the Swiss people and the YMCA."

And the Swiss people did their utmost. At Kreuzlingen all the walking cases from the first train had to wait the whole afternoon in the station. The captain of the Swiss military police had the idea of showing a movie and telephoned Berne to secure permission for the men to walk up through the town to a theater. The American consulate in Zurich phoned the M-G-M agency, which sent down a special film by express. The editor of a local paper produced a schoolgirls' chorus to sing for the men and a high-grade accordion duo, one of whom had to be released from military service for the afternoon while the other got time off from his job in a factory. It was impossible to find an operator for the film projector in mid-afternoon, so the captain himself ran the machine. Of course the show was a success. Some of the men had not seen a movie in years. But the walk through the town, with shop windows alight and things like chocolate, civilian clothes and radios displayed for sale, made almost as deep an impression.

An experience like this brought home to us the penury which characterized life in all prison camps. The greeting cards we distributed came from the printer with a bit of tissue paper between each two; the men saved every piece. In one compartment where eight men were sitting, I asked how they were off for pencils. "Oh, we are fine," they said, "we have two in this compartment."

The men were so delighted to be able to talk to someone in their own language that I decided to accompany the train back to Geneva and spent the eight hours going from compartment to compartment in the train just sharing the almost incredible joy of their freedom, and answering hundreds of questions. What did we talk about? Nothing deeply important or very personal, for we were always surrounded by a group, but we talked of home, and of how often they had letters from there, and of how soon it would be before they would see home again. Men showed the pictures of their wives and children, or photographs of life in camp. All were eager for latest news of the war. One trainload came from a camp right over on the Polish-Silesian frontier and they wondered if the Russian army had rolled over it yet. They kept trying to express their feelings about liberation, but as one man said, "There's just no words for it." Three years before, in the sorting pen at Rivesaltes, I had heard the same phrase, but now it had another meaning.

As we said good-by in the Geneva station, one officer explained to me: "After all these years in camp a 'Kriegie' wonders if he is quite like normal people and if he will know how to talk with folks outside the wire; and just having you to talk with, discovering that you don't think that we're queer or anything like that, has meant more than anyone could say!"

That was the first and last exchange of war prisoners across Switzerland. Events were moving so swiftly toward the German collapse that, what with the demoralization of transport in the Reich and the last futile efforts to stop the onrushing Allies, no further transports came through.

Anyway, it was time to return to Paris. Before we drove out of Geneva that morning, the radio announced that the German surrender was expected, but warned us not to be impatient. It was lovely weather and we drove all that day through new-green crops and familiar towns and villages. Sometime during the day announcement of the surrender must have come through, for all afternoon we kept seeing villagers putting up flags on their houses and gathering in happy-faced little groups at street corners. When we stopped for the night in a tiny hostel in Auxerre (all the large hotels were full of military personnel) we too heard the news: the formal announcement would come tomorrow.

Arriving in Paris a little after noon, we had just time to deposit our baggage in the apartment at United States House and hurry across town to the Palais de Chaillot for the ceremony. The city was a mass of flags of all the Allied nations, and the brilliant sunshine and the almost unbearably intense atmosphere of expectancy nearly made us forget that the war was still far from ended. In the vast auditorium of the Chaillot Palace, the only decoration was a line of the Allied flags across the stage against the dark velvet curtain. The colors, red, blue and white, gold or green, seemed more luminous for this supreme occasion. It was odd to see the Soviet flag, hammer and sickle glowing against a red ground, standing beside our own. For the moment we believed that this heralded new and more friendly cooperation between the two greatest powers in the world. There was a splendid soldiers' choir, an army band, and a dozen chairs for the participating personages.

This was no moment of wild rejoicing; rather, it was a solemn service of thanksgiving and dedication, to mark the end of the war on this continent. There were prayers, the choir sang twice: then came a half-dozen brief addresses and the band played national anthems, one after another. In its simple dignity, infinitely deep and moving, this was a peculiarly fitting recognition of the historic moment.

The Paris sirens were sounding "all clear" for the last time, as we emerged from the profound emotion of that service into a city wild with rejoicing: streets crowded with shouting people, dancing or hugging each other, with tears of joy in their eyes. Trucks and cars, garlanded and beflagged, crowded with singing, gesticulating men and women, created traffic jams at every crossing.

The crowded traffic was like that first terrible day of the exodus, nearly five years ago—but what a difference in our feelings then and now! The sunlit sky was adrone with hundreds of parading aircraft. All that night the streets were crowded. There were marvelous fireworks, and what at first glance might have seemed to be undiluted joy. But closer scrutiny revealed the same undercurrent of sober reflection, the same conviction that so much of the task still lay ahead of us, that we had felt in the Chaillot service of thanksgiving. With a new dedication we set ourselves for the reconstruction years ahead.